the Revolution Myth

by Gene Fisher and Glen Chambers

Based on research from
UNITED STATES HISTORY for Christian Schools™

Bob Jones University Press

The Revolution Myth

© 1981 Bob Jones University Press, Inc.
Greenville, South Carolina 29614

ISBN 0-89084-152-7

Printed in the United States of America

20   19   18   17   16   15   14   13   12   11   10   9   8   7

Contents

Preface
A Chronology of the Era
Introduction
  I. Colonial relationship to Britain
     Parliament 1
     Mercantilism 4
     The King 5
        Policy changes
        Potential tyrant
     French and Indian War 8
     Sugar Act 10
     Stamp Act 11
     Declaratory Act 13
     Townshend Acts 14
     Gaspee Incident 15
     Tea Act 17
     Boston Tea Party 17
     Intolerable Acts 19
        Boston Port Bill
        Massachusetts Government Act
        Justice Act
        Quartering Act
     Quebec Act 20
 II. Colonial resistance to Parliament
     Leaders of resistance 23
     Great Awakening 29
     Loyalty to the King 31
     Olive Branch Petition 33
III. Britain's response to colonial resistance
     Prohibitory Act 37
     Mercenaries 44
     Martial Law 45

IV. Colonial reaction to the Prohibitory Act
    Initial reaction 49
    Declaration of Independence 50
       For foreign alliance
       For the formation of government
       For the prevention of reconciliation
    Relationship of the Prohibitory Act to the
       Declaration 55
    Colonial independence 57
       Definition
       Reluctant declaration
       Relationship to *Common Sense*
       Religious implications
       Legal viewpoint

 V. Neglect of the Prohibitory Act
    Founding Fathers 73
    Colonial newspapers 74
    Early historians 76
    Twentieth-century historians 78

 VI. Conclusion
    Not a revolution 89
    Independence not sought 92
    God aided American independence 93
    Further considerations 93

VII. Documents
    English Bill of Rights 97
    Petition to the King 100
    Olive Branch Petition 106
    George III's Proclamation of Rebellion 110
    An Abridgement of the Prohibitory Act ... 112
    Formation of State Governments 118
    Jefferson's Preamble to Virginia
       Constitution 119
    Declaration of Independence 121
    A Dialogue 125

VIII. Aids
    Comparison chart 129
    Self-examinations 134
    Notes 140

A Chronology of the Era

February 10, 1763—The Peace of Paris ends the French and Indian War and leaves Britain with a large debt.

April 5, 1764—The Sugar Act passes. It is the first act of Parliament designed to *tax* the colonists.

March 22, 1765—The Stamp Act passes and causes widespread resistance to Parliament's attempts to deprive the colonies of their legislative rights.

March 18, 1766—The Stamp Act is repealed and the Declaratory Act passes.

June 29, 1767—The Townshend Revenue Act is passed and places a tax on several important items, including tea.

March 5, 1770—The Townshend Duties are repealed, except the tax on tea.

November 28, 1773—The first load of East India Company tea arrives in Boston in the *Dartmouth*.

December 16, 1773—The Boston Tea Party destroys the tea and angers the British.

March 31, 1774—The first of the Intolerable Acts closes the Port of Boston.

June 22, 1774—The Quebec Act passes and establishes the Roman Catholic church in Canada and the Ohio Valley.

September 5, 1774—The First Continental Congress meets for the purpose of seeking reconciliation.

October 1, 1774—The Petition to the King is proposed.

December 21, 1774—The Petition to the King is delivered to Lord Dartmouth and is received by the King.

April 19, 1775—Hostilities begin at Lexington and Concord.

May 26, 1775—The Olive Branch Petition is proposed by the Continental Congress.

July 8, 1775—The Olive Branch Petition is signed by 49 men. (More than half signed the Declaration of Independence only one year later.)

August 23, 1775—The King issues his Proclamation of the Colonies in Rebellion. (See the Proclamation in the Documents section of this publication.)

September 1, 1775—The Olive Branch Petition is delivered to Lord Dartmouth, but the King does not respond to it.

September 4, 1775—The Olive Branch Petition is published in London newspapers so that Parliament will know about it.

October 26, 1775—George III opens the new session of Parliament by proposing the Prohibitory Act, which will dissolve the ties between Great Britain and the American colonies.

November 28, 1775—The Continental Congress authorizes the establishment of a navy.

December 22, 1775—The Prohibitory Act is passed by Parliament in spite of strong opposition by some of its members. The Act marks the beginning of American independence.

January 10, 1776—Thomas Paine publishes his *Common Sense.*

February 27, 1776—News of the Prohibitory Act reaches the colonies.

March 26, 1776—South Carolina adopts a new constitution in response to the Prohibitory Act. (South Carolina is the first colony to do so.)

April 12, 1776—North Carolina instructs her delegates to the Continental Congress to vote for independence because of the Prohibitory Act.

May 10, 1776—The Continental Congress recommends the forming of state governments because of the Prohibitory Act.

June 7, 1776—Richard Henry Lee proposes that the Continental Congress let the American public and other nations know that the King has made them independent. Recognizing that they are already independent, he also proposes the formation of alliances and a confederate government.

June 29, 1776—The Virginia Convention proclaims that their former connections with the crown are "totally dissolved" as a result of the Prohibitory Act.

July 4, 1776—The Declaration of Independence is approved by the Congress. It states that the colonies will no longer seek reconciliation.

July 12, 1776—The Articles of Confederation are proposed. The colonies had been left without a national government since the enactment of the Prohibitory Act. It is urgent that they establish a confederacy of some type.

Preface

Our interpretation of the history of America since the Separation from England is influenced by our philosophical approach to the American "Revolution." Therefore, we have given this event—the Separation—our close attention.

The historian's view of man strongly influences his approach to the study of history. Either he espouses evolution and humanism, seeing man as an evolved organism in control of his own destiny, or he sees man as the product of a divine Creator Who controls both man's world and his future.

Events do not just happen; nothing in human history is inevitable or accidental. Things happen because men work, sacrifice, and often scheme to accomplish human goals. However, some human goals have often been unaccountably thwarted while others have been miraculously fulfilled. Those who believe that the Holy Bible is the revealed Word of God and that God directs the affairs of men and nations easily recognize the hand of God in human affairs.

Most American colonists accepted this philosophy of history. They strongly believed that adherence to the commands of the infallible Word of God would bring both blessing and prosperity from the Almighty. To them, the foundations upon which they established their institutions were of extreme importance. Those who participated in the events surrounding the birth of this nation recognized their God-given responsibility to formulate a government in line with God's Word.

This study presents the colonial leaders as men unique in the history of man. The dissolution of the colonies' legal position within the British Empire forced colonial leaders to establish a new form of government free from outside interference. Never before had a people been given such an opportunity and responsibility. It is evident that they believed their success depended not only upon their own efforts but also upon their obedience to scriptural principles.

God's requirements of His people are as unchanging as His Holy Word. Many questions that we face today were also faced by those who took part in the birth of our nation. Is our present success because of submission to the leadership of the God of heaven, or is it because of accidental forces at work? Were the methods used to formulate our government based on principle or on expediency? Was our nation born as the result of a revolutionary, disobedient, anarchistic spirit, or was it brought into existence as the result of lawful resistance? Did this resistance conform to the jurisprudence of the day and thus to the teachings of Scripture, particularly Romans 13?

Bad beginnings do not make good results. The Scriptures clearly teach that a good cause does not justify using wrong means. Yet for the past several decades, this philosophy seems to have been the basic assumption behind the teaching and scholarship of our nation's origin.

In contrast, this study presents a differing point of view. Anyone interested in the separation of our nation from England should find it useful. It will serve as a valuable aid to the student and teacher of United States history.

We developed this work while preparing a text for the Bob Jones University Press Heritage Studies materials. It is meant to be used on any level at which the origin of our nation is discussed.

Two self-examinations for the reader are included in Section VIII. One is appropriate prior to the reading of this study, the other following. They will focus attention to what may be a new point of view toward the American "Revolution."

The Authors

Introduction

Final interpretations are difficult to make in any study of history. The following interpretation is not the only possible interpretation of the events associated with the Separation from Britain. Because the position presented here was the one taken by many colonists as a justification for dissolving their allegiance to the Crown, it therefore deserves our serious attention.

The underlying cause of the Separation was a dispute between the colonial assemblies and Parliament over legislative authority; therefore, understanding this legislative conflict is the key to understanding the events of the whole period. The legislative basis for the conflict, although rarely discussed today, is outlined here in selective detail.

This study shows how in recent years information concerning a historically important act of Parliament has been unavailable to those interested in the history of the United States. For years we have been taught that we are the product of a revolutionary generation who, because of religious, economic, and political disagreements, finally (through anarchistic and violent means) tore themselves from a loving and legally constituted government. The details which follow will clearly show this view to be at variance with the actions and the beliefs of those who participated in the "Revolution." In addition, the specific reasons early historians candidly present for the Separation of the American colonies from the British Empire differ from those generally taught today.

This study emphasizes the philosophical and constitutional relationships of the American colonies to the English Parliament and King. For this reason, a detailed review of events leading to the passage of the Prohibitory Act (December 22, 1775) is presented. This study is not an exhaustive treatment of this momentous event (the real birthday of our independence from England), but is rather a presentation of selected incidents and ideas which will acquaint the reader with a viewpoint that has long been neglected.

The American colonists did not revolt against constitutional authority; they did not seek independence from the King of England. The king, instead, severed all ties with his American colonies. The Declaration of Independence was not written to gain independence but to maintain and define what had been forced upon the colonies.

Some Americans believe that our Founding Fathers instigated a war on April 19, 1775, in order to throw off British government, and that the Declaration, approved on July 4, 1776, was a public justification of this overthrow. American Christians have had difficulty understanding why many of our Founding Fathers, while adhering to biblical principles in their public and private lives, could, at the same time, rebel against constituted government. Historical investigation shows that they did not rebel.

King George III

I

Colonial Relationship to Britain

Parliament

Basic to our understanding of the American "Revolution" is the belief of the American colonists that they were *not* under the supreme authority of the British Parliament, but only owed allegiance to the King of England. The colonial charters were contracts between the founders of the colonies and the King. Parliament was not involved. If these charters had been mere grants and not contracts, then the colonists were deliberately deceived, any legal ties were void, and the colonists were absolved of allegiance to the King the moment they landed in the new world.

It must be remembered that—unlike the French and Spanish colonies—twelve of the English colonies were settled by individuals without any aid from the Crown or Parliament. The founders of Georgia had received some aid, and perhaps New York received funds—but only for overthrowing the Dutch. Because of the actions of the British government, by 1776 the colonists could charge English foreign policy with ingratitude as honestly as England could charge them with being ungrateful.[1]

All the charters, particularly those of the New England colonies, granted companies and proprietors full executive, legislative, and judicial authority. Parliament was not involved and the King had only restraining power. The Rhode Island and Connecticut charters did not even involve the King. They were contracts between the people and God, establishing independent governments based upon God's Word.

The First Charter of Virginia (April 1606) reads in Article XV:

> The said several colonies and Plantations shall HAVE and enjoy all Liberties, Franchises, and Immunities, within any of our other Dominions, to all Intents and Purposes, as if they had been abiding and born, within this our Realm of England.[2]

It is clear that the Virginians were to be autonomous in their government. Article XVII makes it understood that the colonists were to make and execute their own laws:

> It shall be lawful to us [the settlers] to put the said Person or Persons, having committed such Robbery or Spoil ... out of our allegiance and Protection.[3]

The Second Charter of Virginia (June 1609) in Article XVI specifies that the colonial assembly had legislative and judicial responsibility:

> A General Assembly of the Adventurers, with the consent of the greater part, upon good cause [is authorized] to disfranchise, and put out any Person or Persons.[4]

Further, Article XIX of the Second Charter clearly states that all inhabitants were to be free from Parliamentary taxes forever:

> [The inhabitants] shall be free from all subsidies and customs in Virginia for the Space of one and twenty years, and from *all* [emphasis added] taxes and Impositions, for ever upon any Goods or Merchandise, at any time or times hereafter, either upon Importation thither, or Exportation from thence.[5]

The Third Charter of Virginia (March 1612) in Article VIII gave the colonial council the right to make laws as they saw fit, "So always, as the same be not contrary to the Laws and Statutes of this our Realm of England."[6]

The Ordinance of Virginia was written in August 1621, a direct result of the meeting of the first representative assembly in 1619. Article II provided for two supreme legislative councils. Article VI made it clear that all legislative authority was to come from the colonial assembly. The only restriction was a veto by the General Quarter Court (which was to be dissolved when the colonial assembly had been "well framed, and settled accordingly").[7] Clearly, the colonists in Virginia were to make and enforce their own laws.

The First Charter of Massachusetts (March 1629) is even more specific:

> And wee doe ... grant ... that it shall ... be lawfull to and for the Governor and such of the Assistants and Freemen of the said Company ... as shalbe assembled in any of their General Courts aforesaide ... from tyme to tyme to make, ordaine, and establish all manner of wholesome and reasonable order, laws, statutes, and ordinances, directions, and instructions not contrarie to the lawes of this our realme of England.[8]

The Charter of Maryland (June 1632) in Article VII granted to Lord Baltimore and his heirs

> free, full and absolute Power ... to ordaine, Make, and Enact LAWS of what kind soever, according to their sound Discretion.[9]

The Fundamental Orders of Connecticut (January 1638) was a contract before "allmighty God" and did not even involve the King—certainly not the Parliament. Article VIII says that the "deputyes shall have the power of the whole Town to Give their voats and allowance to all such laws and orders as be for the publicke good."[10]

Similarly, the Fundamental Orders of New Haven gave full legislative power to the colonial assembly and involved neither the King nor Parliament. (Like all the charters in New England, New Haven's legislation sought to fulfill the request that "we would all of us be ordered by those rules which the scripture holds forth to us.")[11]

The Charter of Connecticut (May 1662) also gave the legislative power to the colonial assembly and was approved by Charles II.[12]

The Patent of Providence Plantation made Rhode Island's legislative independence particularly clear:

> Together with full Power and Authority to rule themselves, and such others as shall hereafter inhabit within any part of the said Tract of land, by such a Form of Civil Government, make and ordain such Civil laws and Constitution ... as the inhabitants thought necessary.[13]

The first charter to involve Parliament was the Charter of Pennsylvania (April 1681). At that time Parliament was in the process of gaining legislative authority and, in 1688, forced King James II off the throne in the Glorious Revolution. The next year, 1689, the English Bill of Rights gave control of the lawmaking powers to Parliament.

Even in the case of Pennsylvania, Parliament was only to give approval:

> That wee ... shall att no time sett or make, or cause to be sett, any impossicon, customs or other taxacon, rate or contribution whatsoever, in an upon the dwellers of the aforesaid pvince [province], unless the same be with the consent of the pprietary, or Chiefe Governor and assembly, or by Act of Parliament in England. ...[14]

Parliamentary review was to be an additional restraint against abusive colonial taxes in Pennsylvania, not a means of interference in colonial legislation. Parliament gained the right to review colonial legislation but not to originate it. Nevertheless, the colonies accepted commercial regulation by Parliament because it was beneficial and necessary.

Mercantilism

Mercantilism theorized that a nation's wealth was measured by the amount of gold and silver in its treasury. Thus the object of mercantilism was to obtain a favorable balance of trade. In order to achieve such a balance, a nation had to eliminate economic competition from other nations and from its own colonies. Between 1688 (the Glorious Revolution) and 1760 (the coronation of George III), Parliament began to enforce trade regulations (such as the Molasses Act of 1733) throughout the Empire to ensure that colonial trade would benefit England. Few colonists objected to these regulations. Although these acts required that the colonists send their trade through approved British ports, they were not enforced. The failure to enforce these trade regulations has been called salutary neglect.

Because of this Parliamentary neglect, the regulations were easy to ignore. This neglect reinforced the colonists' belief that Parliament doubted that it had the right or means to make laws for the colonies. And since these trade regulations did not threaten the authority of their own local legislatures, the colonists rarely complained.

The King—Policy Changes

In 1760 at the age of 22, George III became king. His mother and her advisor, Lord Bute, convinced George that his grandfather and great-grandfather had relinquished many royal privileges to Parliament. As a result, George determined to regain royal authority. He wrote in 1761 that "the new Parliament would be the King's, let who will chuse it."[15] A struggle for power began. In the first decade of George's reign there were seven different prime ministers: Newcastle, Bute, Grenville, Rockingham, Pitt, Grafton, and North. Unsettled political policies were the natural result of such frequent changes of leadership. American colonists could not secure their future on the shifting sands of unsettled British policy.

George was not a coldhearted, bloodthirsty tyrant. He was a moral, sincere person who wanted to be a good king. Nevertheless, he intended to strengthen the power of the throne, and his assumption of royal authority automatically altered the contemporary political complexion. "George II in 1727 was middle-aged, pragmatical, and Hanoverian; George III in 1760 was young, patriotic, and deeply committed; resolute, idealistic, and opinionated."[16] Moreover, the new King had no heirs around which a faction of opposition could gather.

He did, however, have one notable weakness that affected his relationship with the colonists—he deeply resented personal slights. In 1759 he responded to a slight by members of Parliament: "I would rather die ten thousand deaths than truckle at their impious feet."[17] His extremely sensitive personality, coupled with his desire to strengthen the authority of the throne, threatened Parliament's supremacy. American colonists were victims of the resulting struggle.

Although George probably suffered from a rare metabolic disease, porphyria, which caused him to become irrational during severe attacks, he was not actually insane. With advancing age, the attacks became more frequent and severe. During the last decade of his life (1810-1820) the disease caused complete physical and mental incapacitation, but there is no reason to believe that his sanity was seriously affected prior to the war (1775).[18]

George III's desire to strengthen the position of the established church in England also disturbed colonial leaders. "The Church of England was an essential part of the constitution," George believed.[19] "What the position of the English sovereign was in the eyes of the English Church was sufficiently shown by the long series of theologians who proclaimed in the most emphatic terms that he [the king] possessed a Divine right."[20] George's desire to make his authority absolute required that he also render the authority of the established (Anglican) church absolute in religious matters.

A Parliament threatened by internal conflict, a King weakened by disease and a sensitive personality, and an established church determined to strengthen its position combined to jeopardize colonial freedoms.

The King—a Potential Tyrant

Because the American colonists were not cruelly and violently treated by England, many have assumed that the British government was incapable of cruelty. Yet in Ireland during this same period, the British government mistreated men who sought just and necessary changes. Representatives of the British government executed the Irish without trial and burned and looted their homes. This abuse in Ireland occurred simultaneously with events in the American colonies just prior to the "Revolution."

The situation in Ireland worsened; George III approved a sadistic death penalty for seven Irish rebels: "You are to be hanged by the neck, but not until you are dead; for while you are still living your bodies are to be taken down, your bowels torn out and burned before your faces, your heads then cut off, and your bodies divided each into four quarters."[21] George III may not have been responsible for these barbarous executions. He suffered attacks in 1801 and 1804 that completely incapacitated him mentally, and although there was a period of recovery between the attacks, he probably was not aware of what he was approving. Regardless, the executions were sanctioned by the British government.

Consequently, many Irishmen fled to America and told their story, making the Americans fully aware of the tactics the British were using in Ireland. Therefore the Americans' complaints of tyranny and despotism were justified. Local control of the colonial legislative and judicial systems prevented similar incidents in America. Since British officials controlled the courts in Ireland—as they wanted to control them in America— the British threat to American liberties was real, and the colonial leaders knew it.[22]

In this connection, historian G. B. Warden maintains that the supposedly calm and sympathetic governor of Massachusetts, Thomas Hutchinson, was nothing of the kind. In unpublished letters that Warden found in the *Massachusetts Archives* (volumes XXV and XXVI), Hutchinson recommended the redesigning of colonial governments along the lines of the Irish governments and the prohibiting of town meetings. Warden states, "With each new crisis Hutchinson wrote to England demanding increased arbitrary powers . . . . But even in the calm months, as [Samuel] Adams had suspected, Hutchinson recommended changes." Warden summarizes the significance of these letters:

> It is worth repeating that the vehemence of Hutchinson's sentiments and suggestions indicates an entirely different portrait of the man who wrote a careful history of his native province and to all outward appearance maintained a calm, judicious air. Happily for him, the Bostonians did not know the contents of his unpublished letters.[23]

Warden distinguishes the "unpublished letters" from the nine letters that Benjamin Franklin obtained and forwarded to Samuel Adams. These letters (after careful editing by Adams) were used as propaganda against Hutchinson. Although the nine letters did not justify the colonial opinion that Hutchinson was a tyrant, other letters (of which the colonists had no knowledge) did.

The injustices done to the Irish and the tyrannical attitudes displayed by British governors in colonial America exposed the British government's intention to rule the thirteen colonies as it ruled Ireland. The colonists were prepared to die in order to prevent that kind of rule.

The French and Indian War

The French and Indian War ended in 1763, leaving Britain with a national debt of about £140,000,000, the largest in history. About half of the increase was incurred in North America. Accordingly, Parliament insisted that the American colonists contribute to the expenses of the Empire. The colonists refused to pay, insisting that they had already contributed their share toward the winning of the war and that since the lands and assets won went to England, not the colonies, they should not be expected to help pay for them. They also refused because Britain had fought to protect her system of mercantilism, not American colonists. Nevertheless, Britain proposed to tax the Americans.

Parliament levied taxes, not to pay existing debts, but to support British troops left in the colonies after the war. The colonists protested that they did not need the army in peacetime. They particularly resented the stationing of soldiers in the coastal cities rather than on the frontier where they might protect the colonists against the Indians. The argument that the army was in the cities to repulse a French invasion did not satisfy the colonists. They knew that the navy, not the army, would defend them against a French attack. Consequently, they reasoned that the army was left in America to enforce parliamentary tax legislation, not to defend the colonists. "The French and their Indian allies had threatened colonial security, but the British seemed to threaten colonial liberties."[24]

A basic principle was at stake. The colonial charters had not given the English Parliament any legislative authority within the American colonies, but after 1763 Parliament began to legislate. By establishing a standing army in the colonies during a time of peace (without the request or consent of the colonial assemblies), the British violated the Petition of Right (1628). In addition, the Proclamation Line, passed by Parliament in 1763, forbade colonists to settle west of the Allegheny Mountains. Despite the merits of this restriction, the colonists renounced it. It violated their charters, denied their claims to western lands, and restricted trade expansion. Most important, Parliament had forced its legislative powers upon the colonists in areas *other* than trade regulations.

More serious threats followed. In April 1763, George Grenville became Chancellor of the Exchequer and introduced his plan for colonial taxation to Parliament in March 1764. Tax legislation challenged the colonists' right to have their own legislatures, a right which had been permitted by Great Britain for 150 years. The colonists argued that, since Parliament could use the army to enforce taxation, any colonial legislation could be counteracted by Parliament's taxation, thus destroying any real independent legislative powers enjoyed by the colonies since the early 17th century.

To organize and manage her growing empire after 1763, England forsook traditional English law and thus promoted the separation of its most prosperous colonies. The Treaty of 1763 led quickly to the Treaty of 1783. The intervening decades were filled with events which clearly revealed God's directing hand in the New World.

The Sugar Act

In April 1764, the Sugar Act stated frankly that its purpose was to increase revenue. Previous regulations had caused little protest because they presented no challenge to colonial freedoms. However, the Sugar Act was different. Based upon the feudal concept of lord and vassal, taxes such as the Sugar Act required—through monetary tribute—colonial subservience to English superiority and parliamentary legislation. Thus the Sugar Act was a direct threat to local control by the colonial assemblies. Pointing to the demise of feudalism in England, the colonists contended that by now they were coequals with Parliament and not inferior in matters within their own colonies.

However, the situation in America was not the King's primary problem. Following the French and Indian War, the Empire was so large that it was virtually impossible to govern. The riots in Ireland and England made incidents in America hardly worth attention. Parliament was nearly at war with itself, and some of the English populace were nearly at war with the King.[25] The colonists believed that, because of these pressures, the Sugar Act did not have the support of the King.

Historian Oliver Dickerson gives the reason for opposition to the Sugar Act:

> Their opposition to the measures enacted after 1763 was not because they were trade regulations, *but because they were not laws of that kind.* They recognized these late acts as revenue laws, and hence a violation of the fundamental constitutional relationship that had been developing through the past century, under which all powers of taxation in the colonies belonged to their local assemblies.[26]

The Stamp Act

The colonists' hope that the King would intercede with Parliament on their behalf soon proved to be unfounded. On March 22, 1765, Parliament passed the Stamp Act, a tax on newspapers, legal documents, and similar articles. George Grenville, who introduced the act, thought it would raise about one-third of the amount needed to support the army in America. The total cost of maintaining an army in America was estimated at £359,000 per year. The proposed tax was mild.

Nevertheless, intense opposition to the Stamp Act forced its repeal on March 18, 1766, less than five months after it took effect on November 1. Opposition flared because the colonists opposed legislative usurpation by Parliament (especially attempts to raise revenue). The Colonists were not asked to pay more tax than citizens of England. And colonists were more prosperous than the English, but in 1764 the average Englishman paid fifty times the taxes the average American paid.[27] Neither were they asked to pay higher taxes than ever before. The colonists had paid five times more in 1698; however, then they did not complain because their own assemblies taxed them. Thomas Fleming observes, "Recent studies have demonstrated that British taxes cost the average American in 1776 about $1.20 a year. Men do not charge cannon under the banner of 'Victory or Death' to save a dollar twenty a year."[28] The colonists pointed out that the King's annual allowance was about £900,000 and that, if Parliament insisted on having an army in America, they could finance it by being more frugal in England.[29] The King used much of the £900,000 to "buy" the votes of the members of Parliament. Through this means he gained support for his programs. Fleming again remarks, "George III had reduced Parliament from a working partner to an obedient servant."[30]

From 1765 through 1774, Britain collected a total of £342,846 from the American colonies. This total for ten years was only a little over one-third of the King's allowance per year. It is not surprising that the colonists, being free from expensive bureaucratic governments, were generally unsympathetic. They knew that Britain's goal in taxing them was not merely for the purpose of retiring her national debt.

The issue was not *how much* money, but *who* requested it. Dickerson explains that the continental colonies were generally prosperous, and their boasting caused envy among their relatives in Britain.[31] Similarly, Britain's persistence in tax legislation was *not* caused by immediate economic pressures. Britain's attitude proved that the real issue was the subjection of the colonial legislatures, not the balancing of the British budget. It is hard to believe that Britain would spend £8,000 to collect £2,000 in New York if her goal were to balance the imperial budget. It is even more incomprehensible that Britain would wage a war costing several times more than the French and Indian War if immediate economic pressures were the primary cause. Parliament's real interest was in the future value of the colonies, which it intended to govern for England's benefit.

Grenville had been warned that the Stamp Act would arouse opposition, but he persisted in encouraging its passage. Nothing could have unified opposition to tax legislation more effectively than the Stamp Act. It affected both the political and religious leaders, especially lawyers, publishers, and ministers, who were particularly able to rally colonial opposition. When Parliament did not respond to their protests, the colonists fasted, petitioned, and boycotted.

Another myth taught us is that the Stamp Act triggered events that led to the "Revolution." Standard reference works repeatedly mention and dwell upon the Stamp Act. Although historians discuss it at length, colonial literature rarely presents it as a spark that ignited a revolution. Colonists instead attacked later acts that involved basic principles and that had not been repealed. The Quebec and Prohibitory Acts were named consistently as the reasons that attachment to Britain was no longer possible.

The Declaratory Act

The real issue became clear when the Stamp Act was repealed on March 18, 1766. Most colonists realized that the repeal was not a concession to the legislative rights of the colonies but the result of the colonial boycott. "They knew that their prayers and petitions had *in themselves* gone unheeded, and that what had counted most in causing Parliament to rescind the Stamp Act was not the truth of the continental cause, not a regard for the constitutional rights of Englishmen who happened to live three thousand miles from Home, but the noise made by the English merchants."[32] The effectiveness of the boycott, not a change in Parliament's attitude, had caused the repeal. At the same time that it repealed the Stamp Act, Parliament also passed the Declaratory Act, which claimed the right of King and Parliament "to bind the colonies and people of America ... in all cases whatsoever" (including matters of religion). Parliament made clear its intention to subjugate the colonial legislatures. However, it made little effort for a while to carry out the act, and consequently, few colonists continued to protest. On the whole, the colonists believed that Parliament had acknowledged that it did not have the right to tax the colonists and that the Declaratory Act was merely a face-saving measure. Chief among those who realized that the critical issue of legislative rights had not been resolved, only postponed, was Samuel Adams.

To those who see America's separation from England as a revolution, Adams is a paradox. He is reputed to be a revolutionary leader in Boston, but he had Bible readings with his family every night and regularly attended church services.[33] He supposedly engineered a revolution, but could not operate a business successfully. He reputedly wanted to overthrow the British government to gain political fame; although he served as Governor of Massachusetts, his political reputation after the signing of the Declaration of Independence was negligible. Further, there is no indication that any of his efforts were made for personal financial gain. Perhaps he was what he claimed to be—a man convinced that liberty was precious and who feared that the British Parliament might usurp colonial freedoms.

Adams did not understand, however, that even a sacred cause does not justify wrongdoing. Although often accused of being responsible for incidents over which he had no control, he probably was responsible for the Boston Tea Party and other irresponsible events in Boston.

The Townshend Acts

Charles Townshend replaced Grenville as head of the British treasury in 1766 and immediately proposed ways of collecting taxes from the colonies. Townshend argued that Parliament had the right to tax America and that America should accept taxation gladly. He gave no legal reasons for his belief, but said that since the colonies had been "planted with so much tenderness, governed with so much affection, and established with so much care and attention," they owed submission to Parliament. A member of Parliament, Isaac Barre, retorted:

> We did not plant the colonies. Most of them fled from oppression. They met with great difficulty and hardship, but as they fled from tyranny here they could not dread danger there. They flourished not by our care but by our neglect. They have increased while we did not attend to them. They shrink under our hand.[34]

In June 1767, Parliament passed the Townshend Revenue Act. It levied taxes on several important items, including tea. It also authorized the use of search warrants by customs officials. The general reaction to this and other of the Townshend Acts is expressed by John Dickinson, writer of the famous *Letters From a Farmer in Pennsylvania to Inhabitants of the British Colonies:* "If Great Britain can order us to pay what taxes she pleases before we take them away, or when we land them here, we are as abject slaves as France or Poland can show."[35] Poland had recently lost her independence, and France's inhabitants were suffering under a tyrannical church and government. The reference to England's old enemy, France, was particularly galling because Britain had long contrasted her government to France's with pride. Dickinson was not a radical. He was so opposed to violent resistance that he refused to sign the Declaration because he thought that it was premature and that reconciliation might still have been possible. Nevertheless, he wholeheartedly denounced British taxation.

In addition, the Townshend Acts provided that Parliament, not the colonists, would pay the governors and other officials. The colonists would lose control of the "purse strings" of government. Historian Neil R. Stout has noted, "The real purpose of the Townshend Acts was to establish precedents by which the constitutional issue would be resolved in favor of Parliament, and that is what the Americans feared."[36] Townshend justified the colonists' contention that larger taxes would follow if they conceded the right to tax by saying, "There is no telling where it [taxation] might stop."[37] The real reason for the Townshend Acts was to exert Parliament's lawmaking authority over the internal affairs of the colonies. Once that authority had been forced upon the Americans, the British government could tax as much as it wanted.

In spite of the serious consequences of the Townshend Acts, opposition was not especially strong until Britain sent additional troops to Boston in 1768. More troops alarmed the colonists and renewed opposition; consequently, the acts were repealed on March 5, 1770. The tax was retained on one item, tea—not for the sake of revenue but to reaffirm Parliament's supposed supremacy.

The *Gaspee* Incident

The Townshend Acts were repealed the same day the Boston Massacre occurred. As a result of the Massacre, the British troops were moved outside the town. From that time until the Boston Tea Party in December of 1773, there was only one incident that, according to the British, marred relations between the colonies and England. An armed customs ship, the *Gaspee,* ran aground off the coast of Rhode Island. Rhode Island merchants and sailors overpowered the crew and burned the ship. No one was killed or seriously injured.

Although burning the ship was an illegal, irresponsible act, British customs crews, like the one on the *Gaspee,* also committed many immoral, illegal acts in the process of collecting revenues. They often confiscated for their own personal use sailors' personal belongings and other valuables from the ships under inspection. This outright piracy was "legal" because it was committed by government officials. Like the publicans of New Testament times, these officials were hated. The destruction of the *Gaspee* was wrong, but in light of the conduct of the customs officials, it was not surprising.

Although the *Gaspee* incident was the only significant incident in *three years,* the troops remained near Boston and other coastal towns. For three years General Gage wrote to Barrington, Great Britain's Secretary of War, and reluctantly admitted that the colonies were peaceful. Barrington recommended the removal of *all* troops from America.[38] (Most of the troops had already been removed from the frontier forts.) The troops were neither removed nor reduced along the coast. The reason was obvious: the troops were there to enforce Parliament's sovereignty. They could not have been there to quiet a general rebellion because there was none. Certainly the *Gaspee* incident did not justify continuing the military occupation.

The colonists had accepted the tax on tea so that Britain could save face. After three years they believed the tax issue dead. (The East India tea monopoly would raise it again.) Failing to see any other reason for the presence of the troops, the colonists concluded that they were there to enforce the right of Parliament to tax the colonies and that a tea tax would be used to pressure them to acknowledge that right.

John Shy, in an authoritative work on the British army in America, concludes that a major reason for keeping troops in America was to enforce British legislation. Although he also recognizes accompanying considerations, the defense of the colonists, as such, was not a major one.[39]

The Tea Act

Samuel Adams and others continued to demand the removal of the tax on tea because it remained a challenge to the legislative rights of local colonial assemblies. Adams summed up the conflict: "The power assumed and exercised by the British Parliament is, in truth, the foundation of the grievance. We have petitioned against it; and if we admit that they have the right, we have no ground of complaint."[40] Adams, of course, did not admit the right, nor did the majority of the colonists. An article in an English newspaper in 1768 said that even in England nine out of ten persons believed that the Americans had right on their side.[41] In spite of the colonists' belief that the tax was illegal, the protests of Samuel Adams, and the "smuggled" tea from Holland, many colonists paid taxes on English tea and drank it for the next three years. The colonists viewed the repeal of the Townshend Acts as a concession to the colonists' right to maintain the independence of their own legislatures. The retained tea tax was only another face-saving measure, the colonists believed.

Then, on May 10, 1773, Parliament granted a monopoly to the corrupt and nearly bankrupt East India Tea Company. Quality tea would be offered to the Americans at a *bargain* price. Even including the tax, the tea was cheaper than what could be smuggled from Holland. What the British claimed was an effort to save the East India Company was, to the colonists, an effort to entice Americans to acknowledge the legislative authority of the British Parliament. Benjamin Franklin reported that the British ministry believed that threepence on a pound of tea would "be sufficient to overcome all the patriotism of an American."[42]

The Boston Tea Party

The *Dartmouth,* first of the tea-laden ships, arrived at Boston on November 28, 1773. The Patriots immediately placed it under guard to prevent it from being unloaded since customs laws demanded that taxes be paid on all unloaded goods. Moreover, if the tea were not unloaded within twenty days, it would be auctioned (an action the Patriots hoped to prevent also, because the taxes would still have to be paid). Efforts were made to have the tea returned, but the Massachusetts governor, Thomas Hutchinson, was determined that it would not be returned.

The twenty days expired at midnight on December 16, 1773. On that evening after a meeting of about 6,000 townspeople in the Old South Meeting House, the Boston Tea Party took place. A group of perhaps 150 men and boys—some disguised as Indians, others crudely disguised with only soot and hats to cover their faces, and some undisguised—quietly and quickly boarded the *Dartmouth* and two other newly arrived ships. Among the participants, Paul Revere was the only famous American known to have been there. The crews of the three ships were locked in the holds, and in less than three hours 342 cases of tea were dumped into the harbor. Hardly a word was spoken by either the participants or by the large crowd that watched from the wharf. At low tide the tea piled up beside the ship, so it was necessary to scatter it in the water. The men avoided damaging anything except the tea. A broken padlock was anonymously replaced the next day. After carefully cleaning the ships, replacing everything, and taking food and drink to the released crews, the participants lined up at attention on the wharf. They emptied the tea from their shoes and swept it into the harbor. Only one man was injured, and only one man was caught stealing tea.

The Boston Tea Party was intended as a resistance to illegal usurpation by Parliament. Although the principle that the participants were defending was supported by most colonists, many denounced the Tea Party itself. Nevertheless, colonial leaders sincerely believed that acceptance of the tea would have meant the end of their colonial constitutions and governments. The real price of the tea was American submission to parliamentary control.

On April 19, 1774 (ironically exactly one year before the Battle of Lexington), Charles Fox, a member of Parliament, summed up the tax issue:

A tax can only be laid for three purposes; the first for a commercial regulation, the second for revenue and the third for asserting your right. As to the two first, it has clearly been denied it is for either; as to the latter, it is done with a view to irritate and declare war there, which if you persist in, I am clearly of the opinion you will effect, or force into open rebellion.[43]

Members of Parliament who had opposed colonial taxation (William Pitt, Charles Fox, and Edmund Burke) believed that Boston should be punished for the Tea Party and that Parliament had supreme legislative authority over the colonists. In other words, at this time the American colonists had no friends in Parliament. The early charters had granted full control of all local areas of colonial life (including religion) to the colonists. When the colonists talked about representation, they did not mean that they wanted representatives from each colony in the English Parliament. They meant, instead, that each colonial assembly should represent that colony in the same way that Parliament represented England and with the same relationship to the King (as granted by the charters).

The Intolerable Acts

Parliament's response to the destruction of the tea was the passage in 1774 of five separate, punitive acts. Individually the acts brought tremendous resistance to English policy. Taken together, they made war inevitable. The acts sought a single goal—complete submission to Parliament through the breaking of colonial will. Parliament's attitude was reinforced by a special election (1774) that replaced several members who were sympathetic to the American complaints. English voters had been angered by news of the Tea Party and had voted into power supporters of punitive action toward Massachusetts. Parliament now prepared to make an example of Boston and Massachusetts. Only in Massachusetts, at this time, were the leaders of resistance to British measures declared "rebels" and the entire colony placed in a "state of rebellion."

The first of these acts became effective on June 1, 1774. The Boston Port Bill closed Boston's harbor until the tea (worth about $100,000 by today's standards) was paid for. In order to enforce this act, the British strengthened their navy and army in America.

Samuel Adams, hearing about the Boston Port Bill, distributed letters to the other colonies asking for their support. A communications network, called the Committees of Correspondence, had been developed in 1772 by the colonial leaders and proved its efficiency by spreading news about the bill in record time. (Over the years, Paul Revere gained popularity by establishing the overall speed record in taking news from Boston to Philadelphia and back.) The other colonies responded sympathetically because they realized that what had happened to Boston could happen to them.

The Massachusetts Government Act annulled that colony's charter in May. On the same day the Administration of Justice Act provided that British officials accused of crimes in Massachusetts would be tried in another colony or in England. In June, further legislation made private homes available for the quartering of British soldiers if no other accommodations could be provided.

The Quebec Act

As predicted by some colonial preachers, Parliament soon passed an act that threatened the colonies' *religious* freedom. The act was so controversial that no member of Parliament wanted to be known as its author. It was a clear violation of the Treaty of Paris, 1763. Yet the Quebec Act became law on June 22, 1774. The colonists named it (along with the measures of 1774 which had been directed against Boston) "Intolerable." Indeed, to many it was the most intolerable because it established as the official church the Roman Catholic church in the newly founded province of Quebec. This act might not have seemed important to many members of Parliament since England had always had an established church. Nonetheless, some members bitterly protested its passage. To the Congregationalists in Massachusetts and to colonists who wanted to deny the privileges of an established church to the Anglicans (Episcopals) in Virginia, its passage was crucial.

Extent of
British →
settlement
1774

Quebec
before
Quebec Act

The Province of Quebec, the vast area north and
west of the Ohio River, was greater in size than the
original British settlements. The Quebec Act thus
allowed Catholicism to nearly encircle the most densely
populated Protestant colonies. Although the colonists
were angered because the Act annulled their claims to
western lands and strongly favored Roman Catholics,
even greater concern was caused by the realization
that if Parliament could establish Catholicism in
Quebec, it could also establish Anglicanism in the
thirteen colonies. Many colonists believed that the
Church of England was about to appoint an Anglican
bishop for the colonies. The bishop, it was feared,
would enforce Anglican authority upon all American
colonies.

Established churches were supported by forced tithes (taxation). Church taxation gave the church political power over the citizen and forced him to support a church whose doctrines might oppose his own beliefs and conscience. Colonists also feared established churches because the government appointed the church officials. To the Bible-believing independents, it was important to have ministers and officials whose duty was to God and not to man. Furthermore, the colonists feared established churches because they controlled the education of young people. Consequently, the Quebec Act endangered the religious freedom for which many had come to America.

Peter N. Carroll has noted:

> Throughout the years of crisis, the American clergy defended the colonial position and insisted that civil liberties were the only bastion of true religion. Without constitutional safeguards, they argued, the episcopacy would destroy the dissenting churches.[44]

The fear of government-imposed religion was the main reason for the protest against the Quebec Act.

The Quebec Act marked a radical departure by England from past colonial policy. It was of sufficient importance for Thomas Jefferson to bring it forcefully to the attention of the world in the Declaration of Independence:

> For abolishing the free System of English Laws in a neighboring Province, establishing therein an Arbitrary government, and enlarging its Boundaries so as to render it at once an example and fit instrument for introducing the same absolute rule into these colonies.

II

Colonial Resistance to Parliament

Leaders of Resistance

The "Revolution" often is pictured as resulting from the leadership of colonial politicians spearheaded by Samuel Adams. This view might account for the actions of the Continental Congress, which began to meet in September 1774, but it cannot explain widespread support for the opposition to British legislation. John Adams, Samuel's cousin, said "that it is not possible to persuade a large people, for any length of time together, to think themselves wronged, injured, and oppressed, unless they really were, and saw and felt it to be so."[1] Widespread support for the American cause sprang from *real* grievances, the significance of which Congregational, Baptist, and Presbyterian congregations learned from their ministers.

By the end of the French and Indian War, most of the colonists attended Congregational, Baptist, and Presbyterian churches. Many of the political leaders were also members of these non-Anglican churches. Most of the preachers in these churches encouraged

American resistance from their pulpits. Consequently, believes one historian, "It can also be shown that American patriots (with the possible exception of Thomas Jefferson) intended to create, and did so, not a secular nation but a Christian nation."[2]

Statements by Bible-believing men in favor of colonial resistance are numerous. Stephen Hopkins, Baptist governor of Rhode Island, called the acts of Parliament tyrannical even before the end of the French and Indian War. Jack P. Greene notes that Hopkins had said:

> The King and Parliament had no more right to make laws for us than the Mohawks . . . nothing could be more tyrannical, than our being obliged by Acts of Parliament to which we were not parties to the making, and in which we were not represented.[3]

The beliefs of men like Hopkins led historian William G. McLoughlin to remark, "If we are to understand the connection between religion and the Revolution, therefore, we must understand not only its political ideology but also the religious ideology of that large body of Patriots who devoutly believed in the Bible."[4] The basic issue for most of the colonists was religious freedom. "Regardless of their own theological difference, the dissenters in the American churches viewed the Anglican Church as the grand enemy of religion."[5] The preachers argued that "the episcopacy would destroy dissenting churches."[6]

Ezra Stiles, president of Yale University, denounced legislation by Parliament because he believed its purpose was to establish the Anglican Church in the American colonies. Historian Peter N. Carroll describes Stiles as being "convinced of the existence of an Anglican plot to destroy colonial rights." Carroll also writes that the conflicts between the Americans and the hierarchy of the English Church "served as irritants to keep the colonists alive to the need to preserve their liberties from what they considered to be demonic threats of England."[7]

Stiles, early in 1761, described the type of association that the churches of New England should have and, in so doing, clearly denounced established churches. [8] He then challenged the pastors of those churches:

> We should often relate to our posterity the history of the wonderful providence of God in the settlement of this country; and remark the growth of our churches, and engage them by all the honorable motives of Christianity to stead fastness in the faith once delivered to the saints, and in the liberty wherewith the gospel has made us free. [9]

Stiles and others placed the colonists' cause above a mere struggle to preserve political and economic liberty.

Jonathan Mayhew, a Congregational preacher from a family that had dedicated itself to reaching the Indians with the gospel for several generations, made the choice simple for his congregation: "liberty, the Bible, and common sense, in opposition to tyranny, priestcraft, and nonsense." [10] Joseph Emerson stated eight years before the Quebec Act his belief that tax by Parliament would lead to the loss of religious liberty. Emerson, also a Congregational preacher, said in 1776:

> For they [the colonial leaders] saw, while our civil liberties were openly threatened, our religious shook; after taking away the liberty of taxing ourselves, and breaking in upon our charters, they feared the breaking in upon the act of *toleration,* the taking away of liberty to choose our own ministers, and then imposing whom they [Parliament] pleased upon us for spiritual guides, largely taxing us to support the pride and vanity of diocesan Bishops, and it may be by and by making us tributary to the See of Rome [Pope] and in a little time we must either have took a wafer for our God and Saviour, and bowed down to a stupid priest, or suffered all those misuses which that persecuting church could have invented. [11]

Samuel Langdon proclaimed to the Congress of Massachusetts on May 31, 1775:

> Because we refuse submission to the despotic power of a ministerial Parliament, our own sovereign, to whom we have been always ready to swear allegiance—whose authority we never meant to cast off . . . has given us up to the rage of his ministers [12] . . . The pretence for taxing

America has been that the nation contracted an immense debt for the defence of the American colonies, and that, as they are now able to contribute some proportion towards the discharge of this debt ... it is reasonable that they should be taxed, and the Parliament has a right to tax and govern them, in all cases whatever, by its supreme authority.[13]

As seen in his message to the Congress, Langdon and other preachers argued the colonial position as effectively as the most eloquent of the political leaders. The preachers, however, made the issue of religious liberty clearer than did the political leaders; they also had the opportunity to speak to the majority of the colonists, an opportunity the political leaders did not have.

Another preacher, Charles Chauncy, expressed in a letter to a friend a general concern of the independent preachers that "missionary" efforts by the Anglican Church had actually been attempts to establish the Church of England in America.[14] Chauncy clarifies the basic motive for resistance to such attempts:

It may be relied on, our people would ... hazard every thing dear to them, their estates, their very lives, rather than suffer their necks to be put under that yoke of [religious] bondage, which was so sadly galling to their fathers, and occasioned their retreat into this distant land, that they might enjoy the freedom of men and Christians.[15]

Other Bible preachers warned that the loss of political liberty would mean the loss of religious liberty. On the whole, the ministers issued the first and the loudest complaints against Parliament's usurpation. As expressed by a New England preacher, Joseph Perry, "of all our blessings then, we should esteem our religious the most valuable."[16] In reference to the Quebec Act, he says:

What a shocking figure must this make in the English annals. And what a stigma of disgrace and inconsistency must it fix on a professedly Protestant Parliament, for having enacted it: When once this source of national and colony woe shall have run its length, where are we?[17]

David Jones, preaching in Philadelphia in 1775, summarized the situation with a touch of sarcasm:

> [Parliament believed] we should give them as much money as they were pleased to ask, and we might raise it in our own mode—Slaves therefore we must be, only we shall be indulged to put on our fetters, to suit ourselves.[18]

His feeling toward Parliamentary taxation was typical.

A majority of preachers in some denominations (like the Presbyterians) wholeheartedly supported the Continental Congress with their prayers and encouragement. The Presbyterians influenced whole colonies. In June 1775, the Synod of New York and Philadelphia issued a "Pastoral Letter" which encouraged full support of the Continental Congress. Parishioners were told to "not only let your prayers be offered up to God for his direction in their proceedings ... but adhere firmly to their resolutions."[19]

It has been argued that without the influence of Bible-preaching dissenters, there would not have been such widespread support of the principles of liberty for which the colonists contended. Stewart M. Robinson found that in Virginia before 1700 there were only two Presbyterian churches compared to 55 Episcopal churches. In 1760 there were five Baptist, 33 Presbyterian, and 95 Episcopal churches. In 1776 there were 90 Baptist, 86 Presbyterian, and 123 Episcopal churches.[20] Not only did the combined number of Presbyterian and Baptist congregations outnumber the Episcopal in 1776, but their congregations were larger. Some historians feel that the consequence weakened Parliament's support. They reason that in 1760 Virginia could not have supported resistance to the British government because most of her people, particularly the ministers, were bound to England through the Episcopal Church, even though many Virginian Episcopals did (individually) support the Patriot cause. In 1776 the proportions had reversed. The Patriot/ Loyalist associations were determined largely by attitudes toward the established (Anglican) church. Those who feared Anglicanism (Presbyterians,

Congregationalists, Baptists, Catholics, and others) generally supported the Patriot cause. Those who were sympathetic with the Anglican Church (like the Methodists) or who feared some of the other sects tended to be Loyalists. Although there were many Bible-believing Loyalists, the more fundamental groups feared Anglicanism and, on the whole, strongly supported the Patriot cause.

> In the end, the Anglican clergy constituted a major group in the Loyalist camp. Among articulate dissenters, however, the colonial position won virtually unanimous approval.[21]

Virginia was important to the Patriot cause, and the independent churches were important to Virginia. Robinson summarizes the influence of new churches:

> The trend of church planting in the three-quarters of the century before the outbreak of the Revolution is remarkable in Virginia in the fact that the period began with an almost exclusive preponderance of Anglican Churches, 'by law established'; it ended with a rush of non-conformist congregations which could not fail to have a profound effect upon contemporary political opinion.[22]

According to one Baptist historian, there were only a few Baptist churches in Virginia in 1760. William Cathcart, in a small book written in connection with the Centennial (1876), said that by 1775 the Baptists had

> now secured so many of the common people in their ranks, and the remainder had become so convinced of the justice of their views about a free state and a free church, that, practically, the Baptists controlled the larger number of white Virginians, whom they led directly into the Revolution; for, to a man, they were in favor of it.[23]

It was Cathcart's opinion that "without the Baptists of Virginia, the genius and glory of Washington might have been buried in the quiet home of an almost unknown Virginia planter."[24]

Great Awakening

The impetus behind the tremendous increase of Baptists and Presbyterians following the French and Indian War was the Great Awakening. And many historians maintain that the Great Awakening was the force behind colonial resistance to Parliament. Peter N. Carroll says that religious attitudes in Revolutionary America still reflected the evangelical excitement of the Great Awakening of 1740.[25] William G. McLoughlin says "that the roots of the Revolution as a political movement were so deeply embedded in the soil of the First Great Awakening forty years earlier that it can be truly said that the Revolution was the natural outgrowth of that profound and widespread religious movement."[26] He explains the reason that the issues were important to individual citizens: "The revivalists were concerned simply and solely with converting individual sinners into children of God. They preached that men were innately depraved, born in sin, and bound to roast in hell, unless they received the grace of God in their hearts."[27]

Historians note the prevalence and the importance of biblical Christianity in America during this period: "The Bible was believed by practically everyone to be infallible."[28] Another notes that "approximately three-fourths of the colonists at the time of the Revolution were identified with denominations that had arisen from the Reformed, Puritan wing of European Protestantism: Congregationalists, Presbyterians, Baptists, German and Dutch Reformed."[29] Many of the political leaders believed the Bible, and the Great Awakening affected even some who did not.

> The revival also touched public figures not particularly well known for their religious activities. Benjamin Franklin, by now transplanted to Philadelphia, was fascinated, if not convinced, by Whitefield's preaching and was his printer in Philadelphia for a number of years. At least two of the revolution's most conspicuous firebrands were also pulled into the revival's sway. Samuel Adams is said to have turned frequently to the works of Jonathan Edwards as a source of spiritual refreshment, and young Patrick Henry was deeply

influenced by the ministry of Samuel Davies, the Presbyterian awakener of Virginia.[30]

The colonists' view of society explains their attitude toward governmental regulation, especially regulation in matters of religion. "Society, they felt, must indeed be transformed by the gospel, but this transformation had to proceed from the supernatural act of God in renewing the individual."[31] This attitude was largely a result of the Great Awakening.

The results of this genuine revival which swept America in 1739-40 lasted for several decades. Its two most famous preachers were Jonathan Edwards and George Whitefield.

Jonathan Edwards, a New England minister, wrote and preached the famous sermon "Sinners in the Hands of An Angry God." His unemotional sermon style and his logical presentation of the gospel resulted in thousands of conversions. Although his preaching was confined to New England, his converts were not. God used this intelligent, unsensational preacher to help accomplish what Edwards deeply desired—a revival in New England.

George Whitefield's personality was not like Edwards'. Whitefield was one of history's great orators, a stirrer of emotions. Edwards was an American with a Puritan heritage; Whitefield had been an unchurched Englishman. They shared one important trait however: both were humble men. And both preached the gospel to great numbers of Americans.

When Whitefield first arrived in America in October 1739, he was 25 years old. He preached in Pennsylvania before going to Georgia, where he established an orphanage. As he traveled, he preached several times each day. Benjamin Franklin heard him preach in Pennsylvania and calculated that his voice could be heard by about 30,000 people at one time. He frequently preached to more than 10,000 people in one service and during his lifetime delivered more than 18,000 sermons. He preached a farewell sermon at Boston in October 1740, to a crowd of 23,000, and as a result many people gave testimonies to their conversion.

In March of 1741 Whitefield returned to England. He made six more trips to America before he died in New England on September 30, 1770. A New England minister, Abel Stevens, sums up his influence in America:

> The Great Awakening here had commenced before his arrival, but it was comparatively local ... Whitefield's coming renewed the revival. In the South, he was almost its only labourer. His preaching ... founded the Presbyterian church in Virginia. In the Middle States, Whitefield's labours had a profound effect ... The ministers in the Synod of New York more than tripled in the seven years after his first visit ... Edwards' labours were rendered general by Whitefield's frequent passages ... It has been estimated that about 40,000 souls were converted in New England alone ... Since that period, the 'evangelical' character of the American pastorate has not, as before, been exceptional, but general. It made personal regeneration a requisite among the qualifications for the Christian ministry ... It introduced the necessary independence of Church and State which soon after began.[32]

Even Whitefield's death influenced souls. A young man who had heard Whitefield preach and had made fun of him was so convicted when he learned of the evangelist's death that he repented and accepted Christ. The man, Benjamin Randall, later became a Baptist minister and founded the Freewill Baptist denomination.[33]

As a result of the Great Awakening, significant portions of the colonial population had become Bible believers by 1775. Because many feared Anglicanism, as indicated by statements of the clergy, resistance to English control was largely motivated by a desire to preserve religious liberty.

Loyalty to the King

The Continental Congress, realizing that the King was its only hope against Parliamentary usurpation, appealed to him for redress from the Intolerable Acts. Americans apparently believed that the King's ministers were coercing him into support of the absolutist Parliament, and they continued to appeal for redress of grievances even after the Quebec Act. The colonists wrote several petitions to the King, but the last two were the most significant. On October 1, 1774, the Continental Congress again resolved to list their basic grievances. The petition was addressed "To the King's Most Excellent Majesty, Most Gracious Sovereign" and was delivered to Lord Dartmouth on December 21, 1774, by Benjamin Franklin and Arthur Lee. It was received "graciously by the King," and he promised to have it presented to Parliament.

This petition objected to some of the acts of Parliament, asserting that the acts threatened the colonists' right to make their own laws. It especially protested the Quebec Act and pleaded for the preservation of religious liberty in America.[34] It also denounced the actions of the ministry,

> who daringly interposing themselves between your royal person and your faithful subjects, and for several years past incessantly employed to dissolve the bonds of society, by abusing your majesty's authority, misrepresenting your American subjects and prosecuting the most desperate and irritating projects of oppression.[35]

It humbly requested the King's attention and assured him that the colonists were "in affectionate attachment to your majesty's person."[36] It expressed loyalty to the King and pledged that "your royal authority over us and our connexion with Great Britain, we shall always carefully and zealously endeavor to support and maintain."[37] Since the colonists held that the King's ministers, and not the King himself, were responsible for the acts, it concluded with sincere wishes for the King's happiness: "That your majesty may enjoy every felicity through a long and glorious reign over loyal and happy subjects ... is and always will be our sincere and fervent prayer."[38]

In February 1775, Benjamin Franklin desired to express in person to George III the feelings of his countrymen. He wrote:

TO THE KING'S MOST EXCELLENT MAJESTY,

The PETITION and MEMORIAL of W. B[ollan,] B. F[ranklin,] and A[rthur] Lee,

Most humbly sheweth;

That your Petitioners, being Agents for several Colonies, and deeply affected with the Apprehension of impending Calamities, that now threaten your Majesty's Subjects in America, beg leave to approach your Throne, and to suggest with all humility their Opinion, formed on much attentive Consideration, that if it should please your Majesty to permit and authorize a Meeting of Delegates from the different Provinces, and appoint some Person or Persons of Dignity and Wisdom from hence to preside in that Meeting, or to confer with the said Delegates, acquaint themselves fully with the true Grievances of the Colonies, and settle the Means of composing all Dissensions, such Means to be afterwards ratify'd by your Majesty, if found just and suitable; your Petitioners are persuaded, from their thorough Knowledge of that Country and People, that such a Measure might be attended with the most salutary Effects, prevent much Mischief, and restore the Harmony which so long subsisted, and is so necessary to the Prosperity and Happiness of all your Majesty's Subjects in every Part of your extensive Dominions. Which that Heaven may preserve entire to your Majesty and your Descendants, is the sincere Prayer of your Majesty's most dutiful Subjects and Servants.[39]

Olive Branch Petition

In spite of the petition "graciously received," war began on April 19, 1775. No one knows who fired the first shot at Lexington, but if not at Lexington, the war would have started somewhere else. The colonists were determined to protect their right to make their own laws and to preserve religious liberty; Parliament was just as determined to usurp that right. Although the colonists had hoped that armed resistance would cause Parliament to withdraw its legislative interference, the idea that the colonists deliberately engineered a war at Lexington and Concord is farfetched. According to the nineteenth-century historian, George Bancroft, the British tried to suggest "that a handful of countrymen at Lexington had begun a fight with a detachment that outnumbered them as twelve to one."[40]

On May 26, 1775, the Continental Congress again

resolved that, despite the hostilities which had begun on April 19, they would send another petition to the King. This petition, the Olive Branch Petition, was prepared by John Dickinson, Thomas Johnson, John Rutledge, John Jay, and Benjamin Franklin. It confirmed the natural ties with Britain and expressed loyalty to the King. Although it requested that the recent offensive acts be removed, it was truly conciliatory.

Rather than personally assailing the King, the petitioners repeated their charges that recent wrongs were the fault of the King's ill-informed and over-zealous ministers. After a speech in Parliament in which Lord Chatham recommended settling disputes between England and the colonies, William Temple Franklin (secretary to his famous grandfather, Benjamin Franklin) noted that

> His Lordship had concluded his speech with the following remarkable words; If the ministers thus persevere in *misadvising* and *misleading* the King, I will not say, that they can alienate the affections of his subjects from his crown, but I will affirm, that they will make the crown *not worth his wearing.* I will not say, that the King is betrayed, but I will pronounce that *the kingdom is undone.* [41]

In the Olive Branch Petition the colonists, for the final time, paid homage to the King:

> That your faithful subjects on this continent request . . . that the wished for opportunity would soon be restored to them, of evincing the sincerity of their professions by every testimony of devotion becoming the most dutiful subjects and the most affectionate colonists.[42]

Signed by forty-nine men (July 8, 1775), the petition represented all the colonies except Georgia. (Georgia's assembly favored the petition, but felt it could not afford to send delegates that distance.)

Arthur Lee and Richard Penn presented the petition to Lord Dartmouth on September 1, 1775. Dartmouth reported that "as his Majesty did not receive it on the Throne, no answer would be given."[43] Since the King refused to respond, Lee and Penn published the petition in London newspapers on September 4, 1775, with an enclosed proof of its authenticity. Its publication forced its presentation before Parliament.

Just prior to signing the Olive Branch Petition, the Continental Congress issued a Declaration of the Causes and Necessity of Taking Up Arms (July 6, 1775). Members of the Congress, believing that their resistance was necessary, candidly gave their reasons. They stated that they did not want independence, but justice:

> Lest this declaration should disquiet the minds of our friends and fellow-subjects in any part of the empire, we assure them that we mean not to dissolve that union which has so long and so happily subsisted between us, and which we sincerely wish to see restored.—Necessity has not yet driven us into that desperate measure, or induced us to excite any other nation to war against them.—We have not raised armies with ambitious designs of separating from Great-Britain, and establishing independent states. We fight not for glory or for conquest. We exhibit to mankind the remarkable spectacle of a people attacked by unprovoked enemies, without any imputation or even suspicion of offence. They boast of their privileges and civilization, and yet proffer no milder conditions than servitude or death.

> In our own native land, in defence of the freedom that is our birthright, and which we ever enjoyed till the late violation of it—for the protection of our property, acquired solely by the honest industry of our forefathers and ourselves, against violence actually offered, we have taken up arms. We shall lay them down when hostilities shall cease on the part of the aggressors, and all danger of their being renewed shall be removed, and not before.[44]

Most historians (particularly progressives) have taught that the American "Revolution" came as a result of years of dissatisfaction with our relationship with our mother country. According to them, Great Britain had set upon a course of oppression and for a century had gradually made conditions more and more "intolerable" for the colonists. Finally, as a result of taxation, commercial regulation, and restriction of religious liberty, the American colonists had had enough. Deprived of their dignity, money, and freedom, they threw off the shackles of the corrupt monarch (existing authority) and fashioned a government to suit themselves, free from externally imposed taxation and the demands of a demented King. A casual reading of those who were participants in the Separation from England reveals that this was not the case. To the student of this era in America's history, this basic question of colonial allegiance is a puzzle. Supposedly, independence was brewing in the American colonies for a century; however, until December of 1775, the colonists, through their representatives in London, were affirming their allegiance to their monarch and pleading with him to permit them to remain his subjects. Any serious study reveals that the concept of independence came swiftly. How then was this drastic change in fundamental relationships accomplished in the mind of the colonist who valued his subjection and allegiance to his monarch so highly? The colonists did not make the change; George III did.

The colonists did not want an open break or separation from England—even after being expelled from the British Empire by the Prohibitory Act of December 22, 1775. Joseph Reed, upon hearing the provisions of the Act, stated in a letter to George Washington on March 3, 1776:

> Notwithstanding the Act of Parliament for seizing our property, and a thousand other proofs of a bitter and irreconcilable spirit, there is a strange reluctance in the minds of many to cut the knot which ties us with Great Britain.[45]

General Washington responded four days later:

> Was there anything more absurd than to repeal the very acts which have introduced all this confusion and bloodshed and at the same time enact a law to restrain all intercourse with the colonies for opposing them? The drift and design are obvious; but is it possible that any sensible nation upon earth can be imposed upon by such a cobweb scheme, or gauze covering?[46]

III

Britain's Response to Colonial Resistance

The Prohibitory Act

During the crucial years of 1774 and 1775, the King's court, Parliament, and England had been wracked with scandals of immorality, gambling, indolence, and suicide. Curtis P. Nettels describes English society during that time:

> The Seven Years' War, with its victories, its profiteering, and its spoils, left in its path in England a course of extravagance and dissipation without parallel in the country's history. A ruling class, imbued with a feeling of superiority ... pursued its quest for pleasure and intrigue, unrestrained by any strong opposing elements within the state.[1]

The country had so degenerated that Horace Walpole commented, "What is England now?—A sink of Indian wealth, filled by nabobs and emptied by macaronis [foolish and pretentious men]! A senate sold and despised ... a gaming, robbing, wrangling, railing nation, without principles, genius, character, or allies."[2]

At a time when England sorely needed virtuous leaders, she was dominated by degenerate and selfish men. Many colonists, desiring to maintain Christian principles and convictions, considered themselves true Englishmen and wanted to preserve the way of life of "Old England." Benjamin Franklin, upon his return to the colonies after ten years in England, wrote of the condition of England in the spring of 1775. Although lacking moral strength himself, Franklin was appalled. He supported the American colonies' resistance to British usurpation because he wanted America to remain free from England's spiritual and moral degeneracy, if for no other reason.[3]

By 1775 the leadership of England had become so corrupt that many colonists believed their stand against the King and Parliament would be supported by the people of England. Apparently they expected the English to revolt against their own leadership when the colonists resisted British tyranny at Lexington and Concord.[4]

The King, however, remained determined to check the colonists' legal rights. From the beginning of the conflict, George III had falsely assumed that the American colonies were designing a separation from Great Britain. He intended to squelch their supposed designs with the threat of war or, if necessary, with actual war. As early as August 9, 1772, he had expressed his feelings in a letter to Lord North, "I have therefore also looked forward to a time of war."[5] By 1774 events in the colonies had hardened his attitudes. In another note to Lord North on November 18, he summed up his policy: "The New England governments are in a state of rebellion. Blows must decide whether they are to be subject to this country or independent. We must either master them or totally leave them to themselves and treat them as aliens."[6] The King's friends in Parliament supported his attitude. King and Parliament were generally united in their conviction that the American unrest should be stilled by force.

Hoping to have their complaints considered and understood, the colonists had resisted the attempts of Parliament to force them into submission. Nevertheless, they signed the Olive Branch Petition in July

1775, seeking to restore their colonial relationship with Britain. But instead of acknowledging that the grievances of the colonies were just, the King issued via Parliament a proclamation on August 23, 1775, that declared the colonists to be in a state of unlawful rebellion.[7] The colonists assumed that the King's ministers had used his name on the proclamation to make it seem official but that the King had not really supported the Parliament. The proceedings of the Continental Congress on December 6 reflected this misconception in its reply to the proclamation, "The name of Majesty is used to give it a sanction and influence."[8] Their further reply made the colonial relationship to Parliament clear:

> We are accused of "forgetting the allegiance which we owe to the power that has protected and sustained us" .... What allegiance is it that we forget? Allegiance to Parliament? We never owed, we never owned it. Allegiance to our King? Our words have ever avowed it; our conduct has ever been consistent with it. We condemn, and with arms in our hands, we oppose the claims and exercise of unconstitutional powers, to which neither the Crown nor Parliament were ever entitled.[9]

When Parliament reconvened on October 26, George III, in a speech to Parliament, proposed to remove the colonies from his protection and to treat them as foreign enemies. Removal of protection would remove the duty of allegiance. The British government understood this basic legal principle. George Grenville, head of the British treasury, stated the matter clearly on January 15, 1766: "Protection and obedience are reciprocal. Great Britain protects America; America is bound to yield obedience."[10]

The King's proposal on October 26 to enact what he had until then only threatened, touched off immediate opposition in Parliament. Members of both houses denounced the current war as a war of conquest that demanded unconditional submission. The first member to respond to the proposal was John Wilkes: "I think this war, Sir, fatal and ruinous to our country ... We are fighting for the unconditional submission of a country."[11] Wilkes proceeded to defend the American position. Before the day ended, nineteen members of the House of Lords had signed a formal protest declaring the war (and particularly the proposed use of mercenaries) despicable.[12]

In spite of protests against the King's speech of October 26, Lord North's Act (as the proposed act was often called) was laid before Parliament on November 20, 1775.[13] The proposed act later became known as the Prohibitory Act. It prohibited all trade with America, impressed American sailors into the British Navy, and made all American ships subject to confiscation "as if the same were the ships and effects of open enemies."[14] In addition, countries and other British colonies attempting to trade with the thirteen colonies would be treated as "open enemies." The Act was a declaration of unrestricted warfare against a foreign enemy—the American colonies.

The Act officially removed the thirteen American colonies from the King's protection, though it was a concept of British government that the ruler provided protection and that the ruled owed allegiance in return. In Article XXIV the Act speaks of territories "continuing in their allegiance to the king, and under his Majesty's protection and obedience" and of subjects "remaining and continuing under his protection."[15] The Act clearly excluded the thirteen colonies from the King's protection by naming them in Article I as open enemies. Thus the colonists did not renounce the King; the King renounced the colonists by removing his protection. Interestingly, the Act preceded the Declaration of Independence by eight months and passed Parliament in spite of the colonial leaders' expressions of loyalty.

Following its introduction in Parliament on November 20, the Act received much opposition throughout the next two months. Article XLIV drew much criticism. Supposedly providing for "reconciliation," the terms of Article XLIV required the impossible: the absolute submission of the colonists to Parliament's supposed right to legislative control.

On December 1 members of the House of Commons again expressed their feelings about the Prohibitory Act. Thomas Walpole said, "It begins with a formal indiscriminate declaration of war against the inhabitants of thirteen colonies, and after authorizing a general seizure and confiscation of their effects, it concludes with a fallacious nugatory [trifling] provision respecting the attainment of peace."[16] The phrase "attainment of peace" refers to Article XLIV: "to afford a speedy protection to those who are disposed to return to their duty, it shall and may be lawful to and for any person or persons, appointed and authorized by his Majesty to grant a pardon or pardons to any number or description of persons, by proclamation, in his Majesty's name ..."[17] A return to duty required recognition of Parliament's supremacy in all cases.

Walpole asked, "But will the offer of pardon satisfy men who acknowledge no crime, and who are conscious, not of doing but of suffering wrong?"[18] He continued, "A noble lord ... has indeed told us, that nothing should be granted to the colonists until they shall have laid down their arms and made an *unconditional submission* to our claims."[19]

The historian Cobbett writes of another member's (Dunnings') feelings concerning the Act: "no one could now be at a loss to know its genuine import. He was one who looked upon it, from the very beginning to be a formal declaration of war against all America." Dunnings said that a "war of the most unrelenting and bloody complexion was meant to be made on those devoted people."[20] Fitzpatrick believed, continues Cobbott, that "he could easily discern that the Bill breathed nothing but war, and that not of an ordinary nature ... it was war of mere revenge, not of justice."[21]

House member Luttrell believed that "if ... the ministerial army should come off with conquest ... the liberties of England must inevitably fall a sacrifice on the American continent."[22] If Britain persisted in the war, Luttrell warned, "there is not one leaf of the olive branch will be accepted of in America, till you have riveted fetters on the last hand that has nerves able to resist you."[23]

Bayley begged members to consider "whether it was not madness to risk so great a loss, and put a nation to so immense an expense of blood and treasure; in order to establish an *unjust* right in America."[24] Folkestone noted "that there were 35 clauses that aimed at desolation, and one only, a single one, that pretended to be pacific." Burke predicted that a "day would come, when the damnable doctrines of this Bill would fall heavy on this country, as well as on those who first broached them, and were the means of carrying them into execution."[25]

During another session, on December 21, David Hartley said that by Lord North's orders

the shedding of the first civil blood was precipitated on the fatal 19th of April ... When the provincials shall hear the fate of their late and last petition, and when they see that all prospects of peace become desperate, what can you expect but that they should exert every power to destroy your landforces in America during the severity of winter, before you can support or relieve them?[26]

In summary, Hartley commented, "An inflexible majority in the Parliament have now declared all America to be an independent hostile state."[27] Mawbey, on the same day, called it a "barbarous warfare, carrying on against the inhabitants of the North American sea coasts."[28] Lord Mansfield, however, continued his warlike attitude toward the colonial position. British historian George Otto Trevelyan writes that Mansfield advised Parliament to

decline the friendly advances of Congress and rely, for the recovery of their American colonies, upon force, and upon force alone. On the third reading of the Prohibitory Bill he bore the main burden of debate. He summed up his argument in an anecdote which soon ran the round of England and America; and able opponents of the Government in both countries took care to extract, out of what was at best a most unlucky utterance, the utmost amount of horror which it was capable of yielding. The relations of the mother-country and the revolted colonies, (so Lord Mansfield declared,) recalled to his mind an address made by a general of Gustavus Adolphus to his soldiers on the eve of battle. "Pointing to the enemy, who were marching down to engage them, he said: 'My lads, you see those men. If you do not kill them, they will kill us.'"[29]

Mercy Warren (wife of Paymaster James Warren and sister of James Otis) writes in her history that the Prohibitory Act, although passed by Parliament, was vehemently opposed by the nineteen lords who had earlier signed the formal protest against it:

> But in spite of protests, arguments, reason, or humanity, the Parliament of Britain proceeded as expressed in the dissent of the lords, to a 'refinement of tyranny.' Towards the close of the year, they interdicted all trade with America, declared the colonies out of the royal protection, licensed the seizure of their property on the high seas, and by an act of parliament, gave the forfeiture to its captors, and directed an indiscriminate compulsion of all persons taken on board any American vessel to serve as common sailors in his majesty's navy.[30]

Lord North and the King's Prohibitory Act jeopardized the interests of powerful merchants in Parliament. Some British merchants opposed the Prohibitory Act because colonial merchants owed them large debts. As a result, Article XXXVIII of the Act acknowledged the effects on trade ("whereas many and large debts are now due from the inhabitants of the North American colonies") and tried to mollify the effects of making those debts impossible to collect.

The merchants understood that if Britain failed to force the colonies back into the Empire, the colonial debts would be legally cancelled. Therefore, regardless of a British merchant's attitude toward the war or George III, self-interest would force him to support British war efforts.

Many members of Parliament recognized the Prohibitory Act as a final, severing act. In December, after unsuccessfully opposing the Act, David Hartley attempted to have the House of Commons adjourned in order to consolidate opposition to it. Following the denial of his request, he expressed his hopes that opposition to the Act by some members of the Parliament would "remain as a memorial, that some of us, at least, lament this *final separation* [emphasis added] of America with an affectionate regret."[31] After the Prohibitory Act, Parliament passed no other significant acts regarding the American colonies, further evidencing Parliament's recognition of the Prohibitory Act as a final separation. (The vote on the Act was 192 to 64 in the House of Commons and 78 to 19 in the House of Lords. Eight peers protested.)[32] In spite of eloquent protests, the Act became law on December 22, 1775, marking the real independence day for the former British colonists in America. Parliament and the King cast out the thirteen colonies from the British Empire.

Mercenaries

The British government, finding itself unable to obtain sufficient troops in Britain to conquer America, applied to several other nations for mercenaries. Most of them firmly rejected the request. However, a few German princes who needed money responded favorably (one was George III's brother-in-law). Some 30,000 men from Hesse and other small German provinces (all were referred to as "Hessians") aided the British in their attempted conquest of America.

The millions of pounds spent gaining the services of mercenaries also enriched the German princes. These purchased troops were not as dependable as the redcoats, and to the colonists they were contemptible. Although in the eighteenth century, mercenaries were hired to fight foreign enemies, they were not used to subdue domestic rebellions. This tactic proved to the American colonies that Britain now considered them foreign enemies.

The hiring of foreign mercenaries by the strongest nation in Europe to quell a rebellion in its own colonies injured Britain's prestige. Those who opposed the use of mercenaries "denounced the measure as not merely cruel toward the Americans, but disgraceful to the English name; that England degraded herself by applying to petty German princes for succors against her own subjects."[33]

The colonists assumed that the Prohibitory Act was the British government's response to the Olive Branch Petition. After learning of the Prohibitory Act, Benjamin Franklin wrote to Lord Howe:

> His Lordship had seen the Resolution of the Congress which had sent them hither ... that America had considered the Prohibitory Act as the answer to their Petition to the King—Forces had been sent out, and Towns destroyed—that they could not expect Happiness now under the Domination of Great Britain—that all former Attachment was obliterated—that America could not return again to the Domination of Great Britain, and therefore imagined that Great Britain meant to rest it upon force—[34]

The King and Parliament had not only declared the colonists to be out of Britain's protection but had also hired foreign mercenaries to conquer them. The colonists quite logically concluded that Britain intended to rule them by martial law.

Martial Law

The Declaration of Independence denounces both the King's and Parliament's abuse of power. The maintenance of a standing army in time of peace violated the English Bill of Rights (December 16, 1689) and was denounced in the Declaration: "He has kept among us, in Times of Peace, Standing Armies, without the consent of our Legislatures ... He has affected to render the military independent of and superior to the Civil Power." On June 12, 1775, General Gage (military governor of Massachusetts and commander-in-chief of the British troops in America) had stated: "The good people of these colonies ... are rebels and traitors." He then proclaimed that he intended to "supersede by his own authority the exercises of the common law ... and to proclaim and order instead thereof the use and exercise of the law martial."[35]

The Prohibitory Act did to all thirteen colonies what the Intolerable Acts had previously done to Massachusetts—it established martial law. The Prohibitory Act superseded the Intolerable Acts but left the Quebec Act—the most feared of all—intact. The American colonists were legally no longer citizens but "foreign enemies." Patriot leaders became "traitors" and, if caught, subjected to trial by military tribunals. (The penalty for treason was hanging.) The Act subjected citizens to arbitrary seizure and arrest. The establishment of military courts suspended jury trials. Article I defined the American colonists as "open enemies" until they were willing to accept a document "authorized by his Majesty to grant a pardon or pardons to any number or description of persons" (Article XLIV). In the eyes of George III, they were rebels until declared loyal, guilty until declared innocent. These exercises of martial law were contrary to nearly a thousand years of English jurisprudence.

Parliamentary legislation only slightly affected British trade with the American colonies. Exports to Britain remained virtually stable, steadily increasing until the war started. The fluctuation in exports from England to the colonies resulted primarily from natural economic phenomena. Particularly notable is the dramatic increase and decrease between the repeal of the Townshend Acts and the passage of the Tea Act. Colonial boycotts caused a sharp decrease in exports to the colonies before the Townshend Acts were repealed, and nonimportation agreements (a response to the Intolerable Acts) initiated a sharp decrease in 1774. War in April of 1775 and the Prohibitory Act in December of 1775 destroyed all trade.

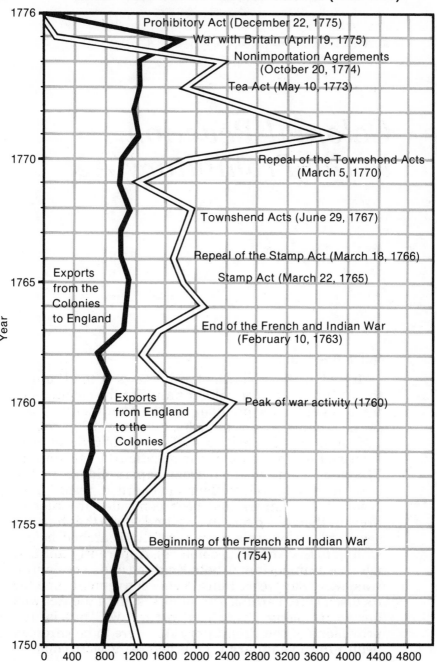

British Trade with the American Colonies (1750-1776)

Year

Prohibitory Act (December 22, 1775)

War with Britain (April 19, 1775)

Nonimportation Agreements
(October 20, 1774)

Tea Act (May 10, 1773)

Repeal of the Townshend Acts
(March 5, 1770)

Townshend Acts (June 29, 1767)

Repeal of the Stamp Act (March 18, 1766)

Stamp Act (March 22, 1765)

Exports
from the
Colonies
to England

End of the French and Indian War
(February 10, 1763)

Exports
from England
to the
Colonies

Peak of war activity (1760)

Beginning of the French and Indian War
(1754)

Thousand Pounds Sterling

IV

Colonial Reaction to the Prohibitory Act

Initial Reaction

It took several months for the news of the Prohibitory Act to reach the colonies and for the colonists to piece together its provisions. The Continental Congress became aware of it by February 27, 1776. In addition, the Council of Safety of Maryland was informed on this date of the drastic new legislation. The news came to them from papers hidden in the bottom of a barrel of flour on board a vessel from Bristol.[1] The papers had been concealed in order to prevent their discovery in England where the ship was searched (all vessels were carefully searched before sailing to the American colonies). Apparently this act, which was important to both England and her colonies, was being suppressed until some convenient time for its disclosure. Perhaps the suppression of the Act was due to its being an *ex post facto* law. That is, the provisions of the Prohibitory Act were to be enforced beginning on January 1, 1776, before the word could be received in the colonies. This incident undoubtedly contributed to *ex post facto* laws being forbidden by our Constitution.

Shortly after February 27, 1776, John Adams wrote to an acquaintance:

> I know not whether you have seen the Act of Parliament called the restraining Act, or prohibitory Act, or piratical Act, or plundering Act, or Act of Independency, for by all of these titles is it called. I think the most apposite is the Act of Independency, for King Lords and Commons have united in sundering this country from that I think forever. It is a compleat Dismemberment of the British Empire. It throws thirteen colonies out of the Royal Protection, levels all distinctions, and makes us independent in spight of our supplications and entreaties.[2]

As seen by John Adams' statement, not only the Parliament, but also some colonial leaders recognized that this act severed the colonies from the King. For the first time, the colonists began to hold the King personally responsible for threatening their liberties. In the first draft of the Virginia Constitution Thomas Jefferson stated that George III

> has forfeited the kingly office . . . And whereas by an act [Prohibitory Act] of the present parliament of Great Britain passed for the purpose of prohibiting all trades and intercourses with the colonies . . . it is declared that the said colonies are in a state of open rebellion and hostility against the king and his parliament of Great Britain, that they are out of their allegiance to him and thereby also put out of his protection.[3]

A few paragraphs later Jefferson writes:

> George Guelp [Guelp was the name of a tyrannical German political faction] having by the said act of parliament declared us in a state of Rebellion and hostility and put us out of his allegiance and after the time of such putting out, ourselves, and the places within our habitation, possessions and rule are not subject to him, and are not to be holden as any of his, nor to his dominion any way belonging . . . also by his own free and voluntary act of abandoning and putting

us from his allegiance, subjection and dominion, may now lawfully, rightfully, and by consent of both parties be divested of the kingly powers.[4]

The Continental Congress also placed the responsibility for the Separation upon the Prohibitory Act. The colonial view that the colonists owed allegiance only to the King is confirmed in the "Notes of Proceedings":

That the question was not whether, by a declaration of independence, we should make ourselves what we are not; but *whether we should declare a fact which already exists* [italics added].

That as to the people or parliament of England, we had always been independent of them, their restraints on our trade deriving efficacy from our acquiescence only and not from any rights they possessed of imposing them and that so far our connection had been federal only, and was not dissolved by the commencements of hostilities:

That as for the King, we had been bound to him by allegiance, but that this bond was dissolved by his assent to the late act of parliament, by which he declares us out of his protection, and by his levying war on us, a fact which had long ago proved us out of his protection; it being a certain position in law that allegiance and protection are reciprocal, the one ceasing when the other is withdrawn.[5]

The Declaration: For Foreign Alliance

Since colonial leaders believed that the Declaration of Independence was merely an expression of an already existing condition, one wonders why it was written. The Continental Congress explained the purpose of the Declaration: "That a declaration of Independence alone could render it consistent with European delicacy for European power to treat with us, or even to receive an ambassador from us . . . ."[6] The Declaration informed other nations of the colonies' independence and opened the way for the requesting of aid.

That it would be idle to lose time in setting terms of alliance, till we had first determined we would enter into alliance:

That it is necessary to lose no time in opening a trade

for our people ... And that the only misfortune is that we did not enter into alliance with France six months sooner.[7]

However, the Americans were a realistic people. Without help they could not keep Britain from conquering them. England's old rival, France, was the most likely source of aid. The Declaration had to be strongly worded to convince France and other nations that America would no longer seek reconciliation with Britain. France was not about to help if America might later resubmit to British control. Therefore, the Declaration concludes, "And that as Free and Independent States, they have the full power to levy War, conclude Peace, contract Alliances, establish Commerce, and to do all other Acts and Things which Independent States may of right do." The Declaration is a diplomatic document, not a statement of revolution.

The grievances listed in the Declaration did not originate with Jefferson. They had been stated frequently from pulpits throughout the colonies. They also had been similarly worded in petitions to the King, but the Declaration (for the first time) directly *blamed* the King. The nature of the complaints makes it clear that the issue was usurped authority. Fifteen of the twenty-six complaints deal with legislation (eight use the word "laws"). Four complain of usurped judicial powers, and seven complain of the misuse of executive authority. Four of the last five object to the provisions of the Prohibitory Act in particular. These last five begin with the statement: "He has abdicated Government here, by declaring us out of his protection and waging war against us." (In an earlier rough draft it read: "He has abdicated government here, withdrawing his governors and declaring us out of his allegiance and protection.")[8]

Jefferson did not exaggerate about the King's abdication. He defined an existing condition that the colonial leaders understood. Americans now read this statement and do not grasp it because they believe that it is a statement of revolutionary propaganda. With regard to the Declaration, Carl Becker explains:

The primary purpose of the Declaration was to convince a candid world that the colonies had a moral and legal right to separate from Great Britain. This would be difficult to do, however many and serious their grievances might be, if the candid world was to suppose that the colonies were politically subordinate to the British government in the ordinary sense. It is difficult to justify rebellion against established political authority. Accordingly, the idea around which Jefferson built the Declaration was that the colonists were not rebels against established political authority, but a free people maintaining long established and imprescriptible rights against a usurping king. The effect which he wished to produce was to leave a candid world wondering why the colonies had so long submitted to the oppressions of this king.[9]

The Declaration: For the Formation of Government

A second reason for a Declaration was to inform the American colonists of George III's action, whereby they had been cut off from all legally constituted government. There was now no sovereign authority in the colonies, leaving the Americans "in a state of nature," without government. The leadership within these former thirteen British colonies now had the awesome tasks of formulating a new government and preserving the people from anarchy.

The Christian should understand that the Declaration (apart from the listed grievances) reflects Jefferson's humanism. It tends to exalt the intelligence and reason of man instead of drawing ideas from God's divine principles. For example, authority comes from "Nature's God" rather than from God, from the "Laws of Nature" rather than from the Laws of God or the Bible. Jefferson described man's equality before the law as "created equal." "Self-evident truths" could be acquired through the intellect and reason rather than from God. Man is said to have certain inalienable rights of life, liberty, and happiness; however, God grants none of these to man, but reserves them for Himself alone. Only when man is obedient to God does He grant a measure of these privileges. The Declaration speaks of government as instituted among men, deriving its just powers from the consent of the governed. Power thus comes from men or the agencies of men, not from God as taught in Romans 13. This false conception of the source of governmental authority is referred to today as "democracy." "Consent of the governed" is often misapplied. The Declaration does not say that "consent" is the means by which our government is to function; rather, it states that this consent is necessary only to establish government. It does not mean, nor did Jefferson believe it to mean, that the people should have a voice in every aspect of government.

There is a mistaken belief that the Declaration set up a democratic form of government. It established no form of government. Government was established by the Articles of Confederation and, later, by the Constitution. The only restriction in the Declaration is that the people should consent to the government that would eventually be established. It does not even denounce monarchies. The Declaration denounced only the British monarchy of George III, which had (by the Prohibitory Act) declared itself an enemy of the colonies.

Representatives from the colonies realized the necessity of stating to the world their independence. The Declaration was necessary in order to secure alliances and to issue a call for the formation of new governments. Virginia, a leader among the colonies, listed these reasons in the *Resolution of the Virginia Convention Calling for Independence* (May 15, 1776):

> By a late act, all these colonies are declared to be in rebellion, and out of the protection of its British crown, our properties subjected to confiscation, our people, when captivated, compelled to join in the murder and plunder of their relation and countrymen, and all former rapine and oppression of Americans declared legal and just. Fleets and armies are raised, and the aid of foreign troops engaged to assist these destructive purposes:
> The King's representative in this colony hath not only withheld all the powers of the government from operating for our safety, but having returned on board

an armed ship ... [withdrawal of governors further suggests that Britain recognized the forced independence]. We have no alternative left but an abject submission to the will of those overbearing tyrants, or a total separation from the crown and government of Great Britain, uniting and exerting the strength of all America for defence, and forming alliances with foreign powers for commerce and aid in war: Wherefore, appealing to the SEARCHER OF HEARTS for the sincerity of former declarations, expressing our desire to preserve the connection with that nation, and that we are driven from that inclination by their wicked councils, and the eternal laws of selfpreservation.[10]

The Declaration: For the Prevention of Reconciliation

There was another reason for an immediate, concerted declaration. Political, economic, and legal separation from Britain demanded such a declaration, but by June 1776, there was colonial sentiment toward reconciliation (as offered in the last part of the Prohibitory Act). Had not Parliament backed down and repealed offensive acts before? Perhaps they would again, some reasoned.

However, colonial leaders perceived that the Prohibitory Act was different and that they had to communicate its consequences to the people. The Act had expelled them from the British Empire; it treated them as a foreign power. The colonial leaders were unwilling to exchange their liberty for George III's protection; therefore, a declaration was needed to make sure that their position did not change. The King and Parliament had expelled them, and now the colonial leadership insisted on maintaining that separation.

Both Parliament and the Crown hinted at reconciliation, but both overtures were rejected. Most of the colonists no longer trusted the British government. Why should the colonists have believed in 1776 that the British government was willing to acknowledge that it had no right to raise revenue in the American colonies when it had since 1763 been claiming that right? The colonists could no longer expect a just reconciliation.

Even later, during the war, reconciliation was discussed. Admiral Howe, one of the peace commissioners appointed by the King (as provided by the Prohibitory Act), conducted beginning negotiations. In September of 1776 the Continental Congress formed a committee to meet with Howe and to discuss possible reconciliation. After the meeting the committee reported to Congress what Howe had said:

> There was an exceeding good disposition in the King and his ministers to make that government easy to us, with intimations, that, in case of our submission, they would cause the offensive acts of Parliament to be revised, and the instructions to governors to be reconsidered; that so, if any just causes of complaint were found in the acts, or any errors in government were perceived to have crept into the instructions, they might be amended or withdrawn.[11]

The committee members refused reconciliation and summarized their reasons:

> We mentioned the repeated humble petitions of the colonies to the King and Parliament, which had been treated with contempt, and answered only by additional injuries; the unexampled patience we had shown under their tyrannical government; and that it was not till the last act of Parliament, which denounced war against us, and put us out of the King's protection, that we declared our independence; that this declaration had been called for by the people of the colonies in general; that every colony had approved of it, when made; and all now considered themselves as independent States, and were settling or had settled their governments accordingly; so that it was not in the power of Congress to agree for them, that they should return to their former dependent state ....[12]

It is interesting to note that still later (in 1778) concessions to the grievances of 1774 and 1775 were offered by the King's peace commissioners in order to effect reconciliation.

The Relationship of the Prohibitory Act to the Declaration

David Ramsay's history recognized the preeminent place of the Prohibitory Act in relation to the Declaration (in the eyes of the colonial leaders). Ramsay, a colonial historian and physician, pointed out that despite the continued hostilities, the colonists' hopes for reconciliation were high, until

that time in 1776, when intelligence reached the colonists of the act of Parliament passed in December 1775, for throwing them out of British protection, and of hiring foreign troops to assist in effecting their conquest .... This act proved that the colonists might constitutionally declare themselves independent, but the hiring of foreign troops to make war upon them, demonstrated the necessity of their doing it immediately .... Some of the popular leaders may have secretly wished for independence from the beginning of the controversy, but their number was small and their sentiments were not generally known.[13]

Mercy Warren also attributed to the Prohibitory Act the responsibility for the sudden change in favor of the independence that had been imposed on the colonists by Britain. Warren described the reaction of the colonists when they learned of the act:

On this information, the indignation of all ranks can scarcely be described. The King's speech was condemned and ordered to be burnt in the centre of the camp at Cambridge. The wavering were resolved, the timid grew bold.[14]

The timing of the Declaration indicates that it was the Prohibitory Act that necessitated the Declaration. The colonists did not learn of the Act until late in February of 1776. Mercy Warren wrote:

The debates in parliament relative to colonial measures, the King's speech, and the rejection of the late petition of the continental congress arrived in America before the month of March, one thousand seven hundred and seventy six. These were accompanied with the intelligence of the Hessian Treaty, and that foreign auxiliaries from various other nations were to be employed in the compulsory system, and that the barbarous strangers were to assist in the entire subjugation of the colonies if not otherwise reduced to unworthy submission.[15]

It was almost the end of March before news of the Act had been widely circulated in the colonies. Apparently the Congress hesitated to make the effects of the Act public because it wanted to give full consideration to the reconciliation attempts of King and Parliament, to establish a unifying government before announcing the colonies' independence, and to make sure of foreign support for the new nation. This hesitancy delayed any resolution to write a declaration until May, and it was not approved until July 4. Considering the time involved to spread the news and to debate the issue in the Continental Congress, the Declaration came as a relatively immediate response to the Prohibitory Act.

That more than half the men who signed the Olive Branch Petition in July 1775, also signed—just one year later—the Declaration of Independence further indicates that the Declaration was a reaction to the Prohibitory Act.

Colonial Independence

The literature of the era indicates that many of the colonists had a different concept of independence from what is often attributed to them. There were several views of independence.

Independence: Definition

To be sure, after 1763 there were a few colonists who desired a complete separation from England and the formation of a government of their own choosing. Some feared that Britain was forsaking her principles of liberty, and they wanted to abandon what they believed to be a sinking ship. They did not hope for justice from the British government. It is difficult to know how many were in this group; Benjamin Franklin, after a discussion with Lord Chatham, wrote that the number of radicals must have been small since Chatham had

> mention'd an Opinion prevailing here that America aim'd at setting up for itself as an independent State; or at least to get rid of the Navigation Acts. I assur'd him, that, having more than once travelled almost from one end of the Continent to the other and kept a great Variety of Company, eating, drinking, and conversing with them freely, I never had heard in any Conversation

from any Person drunk or sober, the least Expression of a wish for a Separation, or Hint that such a Thing would be advantageous to America.[16]

A few colonists wanted independence for personal gain. All societies contain selfishly ambitious individuals, but this sort represented only a small minority of those in colonial America who favored independence.

Most were patriots. They used the word *independence* to define the situation prior to 1763 when they were free from internal British regulation, domination, and taxation. They had enjoyed independence within the British Empire; that is, though they were free from Parliamentary authority, they were submissive to the King.

But even in this last context, the word *independence* was rarely used. Not until after the colonists learned of the Prohibitory Act did they candidly discuss independence, and then as a fact already accomplished by the King, not by the colonists.

Independence: Reluctant Declaration

In addition, Jefferson encouraged an emotional independence from Britain. In an early draft of the Declaration, later rejected by the Continental Congress, Jefferson wrote:

They too have been deaf to the voice of justice & of consanguinity, and when occasions have been given them, by the regular course of their laws, of removing from their councils the disturbers of our harmony, they have, by their free election, re-established them in power. At this very time too they are permitting their chief magistrate to send over not only soldiers of our common blood, but Scotch & foreign mercenaries to invade & destroy us. These facts have given the last stab to agonizing affection, and manly spirit bids us to renounce forever these unfeeling brethren. We must endeavor to forget our former love for them, and hold them as we hold the rest of mankind, enemies in war, in peace friends. We might have been a free and a great people together; but a communication of grandeur & of freedom it seems is below their dignity. Be it so, since they will have it. The road to happiness & to glory is open to us too. We will tread it apart from them, and acquiesce in the necessity which denounces our eternal separation![17]

Jefferson compares the reign of George III to the abdication of James II. "James the IId never declared his people of England out of his protection yet his actions proved it and the parliament declared it."[18] Although James II did not withdraw protection from his subjects, he was deposed for abdicating government. George III's actions made him even less worthy of being king. Further, Jefferson pointed out, George withdrew his protection and thereby legally abdicated government in the American colonies.

The Declaration, therefore, in the name of thirteen unanimous states, proclaims that the monarch who had been obeyed, loved, and honored by them had removed himself from office. George had violated the compact between sovereign and subject just as James II had done, an action for which Parliament had dethroned James in 1688.

Jefferson specified the reasons for cutting ties of allegiance:

> That it was prudent to fix among ourselves the terms on which we should form alliance, before we declared we would form one at all events:
> And that if these were agreed on, & our Declaration of Independance ready by the time our Ambassador should be prepared to sail, it would be as well as to go into that Declaration at this day.
> On the other side it was urged by J. Adams, Lee, Wythe, and others
> That no gentleman had argued against the policy or the right of separation from Britain, nor had supposed it possible we should ever renew our connection; that they had only opposed its being now declared:
> That the question was not whether, by a declaration of independance, we should make ourselves what we are not; but whether we should declare a fact which already exists:
> That as to the people or parliament of England, we had alwais been independent of them, their restraints

on our trade deriving efficacy from our acquiescence only, & not from any rights they possessed of imposing them, & that so far our connection had been federal only & was now dissolved by the commencement of hostilities:

That as to the King, we had been bound to him by allegiance, but that this bond was now dissolved by his assent to the late act of parliament, by which he declares us out of his protection, and by his levying war on us, a fact which had long ago proved us out of his protection; it being a certain position in law that allegiance & protection are reciprocal, the one ceasing when the other is withdrawn:

That James the IId. never declared the people of England out of his protection yet his actions proved it & the parliament declared it:

No delegates then can be denied, or ever want, a power of declaring an existing truth:

That the delegates from the Delaware counties having declared their constituents ready to join, there are only two colonies Pennsylvania & Maryland whose delegates are absolutely tied up, and that these had by their instructions only reserved a right of confirming or rejecting the measure:

That the instructions from Pennsylvania might be accounted for from the times in which they were drawn, near a twelvemonth ago, since which the face of affairs has totally changed:

That within that time it had become apparent that Britain was determined to accept nothing less than a carte-blanche, and that the King's answer to the Lord Mayor Aldermen & common council of London, which had come to hand four days ago, must have satisfied every one of this point:

That the people wait for us to lead the way:

That *they* are in favour of the measure, tho' the instructions given by some of their *representatives* are not:

That the voice of the representatives is not always consonant with the voice of the people, and that this is remarkably the case in these middle colonies:

That the effect of the resolution of the 15th of May has proved this, which, raising the murmurs of some in the colonies of Pennsylvania & Maryland, called forth the opposing voice of the freer part of the people, &

proved them to be the majority, even in these colonies:

That the backwardness of these two colonies might be ascribed partly to the influence of proprietary power & connections, & partly to their having not yet been attacked by the enemy:

That these causes were not likely to be soon removed, as there seemed no probability that the enemy would make either of these the seat of this summer's war:

That it would be vain to wait either weeks or months for perfect unanimity, since it was impossible that all men should ever become of one sentiment on any question:

That the conduct of some colonies from the beginning of this contest, had given reason to suspect it was their settled policy to keep in the rear of the confederacy, that their particular prospect might be better, even in the worst event:

That therefore it was necessary for those colonies who had thrown themselves forward & hazarded all from the beginning, to come forward now also, and put all again to their own hazard:

That the history of the Dutch revolution, of whom three states only confederated at first proved that a secession of some colonies would not be so dangerous as some apprehended:

That a declaration of Independence alone could render it consistent with European delicacy for European powers to treat with us, or even to receive an Ambassador from us:

That till this they would not receive our vessels into their ports, nor acknowledge the adjudications of our courts of admiralty to be legitimate, in cases of capture of British vessels:

That though France & Spain may be jealous of our rising power, they must think it will be much more formidable with the addition of Great Britain; and will therefore see it their interest to prevent a coalition; but should they refuse, we shall be but where we are; whereas without trying we shall never know whether they will aid us or not:

That the present campaign may be unsuccessful, & therefore we had better propose an alliance while our affairs wear a hopeful aspect:

That to await the event of this campaign will certainly work delay, because during this summer

France may assist us effectually by cutting off those supplies of provisions from England & Ireland on which the enemy's armies here are to depend; or by setting in motion the great power they have collected in the West Indies, & calling our enemy to the defence of the possessions they have there:

That it would be idle to lose time in settling the terms of alliance, till we had first determined we would enter into alliance:

That it is necessary to lose no time in opening a trade for our people, who will want clothes, and will want money too for the paiment of taxes:

And that the only misfortune is that we did not enter into alliance with France six months sooner, as besides opening their ports for the vent of our last year's produce, they might have marched an army into Germany and prevented the petty princes there from selling their unhappy subjects to subdue us.[19]

The Declaration's purpose was to inform a "candid world" that an action of the King and Parliament had cast the thirteen colonies out of the British Empire. The document did not proclaim legal, formal severance from England; that had already been accomplished by George III and Parliament on Friday, December 22, 1775.

The colonies, as a result of the Prohibitory Act, were dissolving political bands: "that they are absolved from all Allegiance to the British Crown, and that all political connection between them and the state of Great Britain, is and ought to be totally dissolved . . . ." The Declaration focuses upon this dissolution of "political bands." Certainly the committee members selected by the Continental Congress on June 11, 1776, to draft a document of dissolution (Thomas Jefferson, John Adams, Benjamin Franklin, Roger Sherman, and Robert Livingston) were particular with the wording of the Declaration. These men did not select words implying a dissolution of the entire framework of government ties with Britain (legal, filial, traditional, and constitutional, for example). They dissolved only the "political bands."

The colonists had fulfilled their contract with the

Crown. The moment the Crown removed protection, the obligation of allegiance was likewise dissolved; the contract was invalidated. In a true sense, the Declaration was not one of independence but rather a Declaration of the Severance of Allegiance—allegiance to the King (the only authority by which the colonists had been governed since 1606 when the first colonial charter was granted).

The use of the phrase "one people" in the first paragraph is explained in the last. It was not a declaration of a single, sovereign state but rather a collective declaration of thirteen independent states, each dissolving its allegiance to its former monarch. It was a "unanimous Declaration of the Thirteen United States of America." They were united only in purpose, not in politics. Their only legal connection had been to the King, not to each other. Now that this relationship had been dissolved, they declared (in the concluding paragraph) each of the thirteen colonies to be a separate, sovereign nation. The Articles of Confederation would sanction this argument.

Independence of the individual colonies, which began early in colonial days, continued until the ratification of the Constitution in 1789. This document brought diverse colonies together into a unified whole. The unification of thirteen sovereign nations through the framing of our Constitution reveals the directing hand and grace of an Almighty God.

The colonists declared independence with great reluctance and only as a final resort. John Adams expressed fear of independence in a letter to Horatio Gates on March 23, 1776: "Independence is a hobgoblin of such frightful mien, that it would throw a delicate person into fits to look it in the face."[20] Yet the same letter discusses the Prohibitory Act. Adams was not being inconsistent; he was simply sharing his awareness that independence was a frightening responsibility—especially in the face of war with a powerful would-be conqueror.

Viewing American independence in the light of the Prohibitory Act allows a different appraisal of the

Declaration. The list of complaints in the Declaration is not of revolutionary intent, but proposes to justify America's refusal to seek reconciliation with the British King. The conditions of "reconciliation" required by the Prohibitory Act would have forced the colonists to renounce their right to the liberties for which their ancestors had come to America and for which they had sacrificed during the past 150 years. Such a prospect was intolerable.

The famous resolution on behalf of the state of Virginia (June 7, 1776) takes on an entirely different meaning:

> Resolved: That these United Colonies are [an existing fact], and of a right ought to be [continue to be], free and independent states; that they are absolved from all allegiance to the British Crown [a fact already accomplished by the Prohibitory Act]; and that all political connection between them and the state of Great Britain is [an existing fact], and ought to be [continue to be], totally dissolved.[21]

Because the Declaration of Independence was also intended as propaganda, it is generally concluded that many of Thomas Jefferson's allegations against the King are figurative. This conclusion is invalid. His statements are literal and their meanings become clear as we expand our understanding of the time in which they were written.

Jefferson summarizes the provisions of the Prohibitory Act in the Declaration of Independence:

1) He has cut off our Trade with all parts of the world.
2) He has abdicated Government here, by declaring us out of his Protection, and waging War against us.
3) He is at this time transporting large Armies of foreign mercenaries. [Although hiring mercenaries was not a provision of the Prohibitory Act, George III had been frantically trying to hire foreign soldiers when he proposed it. The Prussian mercenaries were hired specifically to fight American colonists, and Jefferson obviously links their use with the Prohibitory Act. Colonists apparently

doubted that the British would have used mercenaries against them without first declaring them to be enemies in the Prohibitory Act.]

4) He has constrained our fellow Citizens taken Captive on the high Seas to bear Arms against their Country, to become the executioners of their friends and Brethren, or to fall themselves by their Hands. [Because of this provision the act was often called the Restraining or Capture Act.]

Independence: Relationship to *Common Sense*

Some believe that Thomas Paine, a middle-aged infidel, a failure at everything he had attempted, and a schoolboy in the study of government, was primarily responsible for unifying the people of the colonies in the struggle for independence. Yet a reading of *Common Sense* shows its basic thesis to be repulsive to the people, because it was really an argument for war. Although it presents a dramatic case against George III, statements by our colonial leaders present entirely different reasons for refusing reconciliation.

Realizing the impact that the Prohibitory Act had upon colonial thinking puts the value of Thomas Paine's *Common Sense* in proper perspective. Paine completed his pamphlet on January 10, 1776, and by the time it was distributed, knowledge of the Prohibitory Act had also spread (despite apparent efforts by the Continental Congress to prevent it). John Adams knew of the Act before he received a copy of *Common Sense*. Adams conceded to his wife, Abigail, that the pamphlet might be useful in encouraging the Americans, but his general opinion of Paine and his pamphlet was derisive.[22] We should not expect colonial Christians to have been repulsed by Paine's agnosticism since Paine was unknown to most colonists when he wrote *Common Sense*. His agnostic views were expressed later in the *Age of Reason,* not in *Common Sense*. Indeed, *Common Sense* was a stirring expression of many of the colonial ideals in a style that even the relatively uneducated could appreciate.

Although Paine's pamphlet helped to excite the people against Britain and the King, it was not the cause of the Declaration. Colonial opposition to independence from the King appears to have been so general that it is doubtful that the persuasion of Thomas Paine and others could have consolidated the colonists in favor of independence. They were willing to resist Parliament's usurpation of authority because their freedoms were at stake, but they were unwilling to sever royal attachments.

The people had read copies of the King's speech and had heard about the Prohibitory Act discussions in Parliament before *Common Sense* was distributed. News of the Act made a just reconciliation appear impossible. *Common Sense,* consequently, was widely read although it might not have become popular had it not been for the Prohibitory Act. Indeed, it might not have received the prominence that it did had it not been published on the same day that the King made his speech denouncing the American "Revolution." George III himself made *Common Sense* a great topic of discussion.[23]

Independence: Religious Implications

Of special significance to many colonists were the religious implications of the Prohibitory Act. It was an even greater threat than the Quebec Act, since the "reconciliation" terms of the Prohibitory Act would have allowed Parliament to make the Anglican Church the established church in America, as it was in England. Although England was one of the centers for the spread of the Bible doctrine of "justification by faith," at the time of the "Revolution" that doctrine was being denounced, and its preachers persecuted by the High Anglican Church. Consequently, many colonists believed that their most cherished liberty— religious liberty—was in more danger after the enactment of the Prohibitory Act than ever before.

The spiritual and moral deterioration of Great Britain's leadership was proclaimed by a member of Parliament, Dr. Richard Price, in 1776. He wondered why the British Army seemed unable to defeat what some British called an "army of cowards" in spite of Parliament's bringing upon them an army of French Papists [by the Quebec Act], and instigating Indians and slaves, and hiring Russians and Germans . . . it would become us to turn our thoughts to Heaven. This is what our brethren in the colonies are doing. From one end of North America to the other, they are Fasting and Praying. But what are we doing? Shocking thought! We are ridiculing them as *Fanatics,* and scoffing at religion . . . .[24]

The religious motivation for liberty was evident even in the seal which was proposed for the new nation. In the *Report on a Seal for the United States, with Related Papers,* presented to the Continental Congress on August 20, 1776, Benjamin Franklin proposed:

Moses standing on the Shore, and extending his Hand over the Sea, thereby causing the same to overwhelm Pharoah who is sitting in an open Chariot, a Crown on his Head and a Sword in his Hand. Rays from a Pillar of Fire in the Clouds, reaching to Moses, to express that he acts by Command of the Deity.[25]

Franklin wanted to commemorate George III's (Pharaoh's) tyranny in approving the Prohibitory Act by making Exodus 11:1b a part of the national seal: "Afterwards he will let you go hence; when he shall let you go, he shall surely thrust you out hence altogether."

Independence: From a Legal Viewpoint

To many unconverted, pragmatic colonists, independence was necessary and therefore rationally justified. They were unconcerned about whether or not their resistance to England or their independence from England was legal. But to Christians who believed and obeyed Romans 13, rebellion against constituted authority would be unjust. To them, as well as to other people of principle, the legality of their resistance was of the utmost importance.

Judge William Henry Drayton of South Carolina effectively presented the legal considerations of independence. His legal justification for forming a state government independent of Britain is irrefutable. In his mind, there was never any question as to South

Carolina's right to form an independent government. Further, after learning of the Prohibitory Act, he believed that reconciliation was impossible.

Nonetheless, South Carolina followed the leading of the Continental Congress in leaving the door open to possible reconciliation. After receiving the Proclamation (August 23, 1775) and the "royal speech in Parliament" (October 26), the South Carolina Assembly considered the Congress's resolution of November 4, 1775. The resolution had recommended that South Carolina form a representative government "if they think it necessary." The abdication of the King's Governor, William Campbell, forced South Carolina into a state of non-constituted government. Campbell had taken the Great Seal of the colony with him to England, and, as a result, all future acts of the assembly, in the eyes of George III, became illegal. The governors of Virginia, New York, and North Carolina had done likewise.

Judge Drayton argued that the removal of the governor and the seal of South Carolina abdicated the King's authority and removed his protection from the colony. Consequently, South Carolina was absolved of allegiance to its monarch. Therefore, the assembly's consideration, beginning March 15, 1776, of a temporary constitution was justified. Drayton's son related the progress of the provincial congress in memoirs about his father:

> After this manner, the Provincial Congress continued to advance, step by step; daily meeting with oppositions in adjusting the constitution, and striving to surmount them; when on the 21st of March, an act of the British Parliament passed December 21st, 1775, authorizing the capture of American vessels and property, and of which the patriotic authorities of Georgia had become possessed (together with an accompanying letter to Governor Wright, who had fled from that Colony), was transmitted to the Congress, by express from Savannah. [It had arrived in Savannah on March 13.] This, silenced in a great measure, the moderate men, who wished a reconciliation with Great Britain—put down attempts of postponement, and opposition—and greatly

advanced the public measures which were then in hand.[26]

South Carolina immediately reacted to the Prohibitory Act by adopting a new constitution (two days later). The colony also retaliated by confiscating a British ship. The sugar on board was sold and the proceeds placed in the colonial treasury. This act was a reciprocal act of war and would have been unthinkable prior to knowledge of the Prohibitory Act (which was recognized by the colonists as a declaration of war). The door to reconciliation began to close.

But in spite of the formation of an independent state government, South Carolina still hoped for reconciliation. The preamble of the new constitution stated that the government was formed only . . .

> until an accommodation of the unhappy differences between Great Britain and America can be obtained (an event, which though traduced and treated as rebels, we still earnestly desire) some mode should be established by common consent. . . for regulating the internal polity of this Colony.[27]

The South Carolina constitution makes it clear that they did not want independence but that George III had forced it upon them.

South Carolina adopted its constitution on March 26, 1776. It listed justifications for the adoption of an independent government: the false claims of the Declaratory Act, the revenue acts, the royal snubs of colonial petitions, the abuses resulting from the navigation acts, the Intolerable Acts, the Quebec Act, the despotic military occupation of Massachusetts, the unnatural war, the incitement of Indians and slaves, and lastly, the Prohibitory Act.

After becoming Chief Justice of South Carolina, Drayton gave his first address to the colonial Grand Jury on April 23, 1776. He reviewed the charges against George III and concluded

> that the law of the land authorized him to declare, and, that it was his duty to declare, that George the Third, King of Great Britain, had abdicated the government;

and, that the throne was thereby vacant: THAT IS, HE HAS NO AUTHORITY OVER US, *and* WE OWE NO OBEDIENCE TO HIM. [28]

In another speech to the Grand Jury on May 2, 1776, Drayton again reviewed the charges which the South Carolina constitution had brought against the British government. On this occasion, he vehemently denounced the Prohibitory Act:

—Oh, Almighty Director of the Universe! what confidence can be put in a government ruling by such Engines, and upon such principles of unnatural destruction!—A government, that on the 21st day of December last, made a law, *ex post facto* to justify what had been done, not only without law, but in its nature unjust. . . . The world, so old as it is, heretofore had never heard of so atrocious a procedure: it has no parallel in the registers of tyranny. [29]

Drayton then compared George III's offenses to James II's. He reminded the Grand Jury that the famed Blackstone had viewed James II's actions as an abdication. [30] Drayton concludes:

It is as clear as the sun in meridian, that George III has injured the Americans, at least as grievously as James II injured the people of England: but that James did not oppress these in so *criminal* a manner as George has oppressed the Americans. [31]

Despite Britain's efforts to "enslave America," Drayton confirmed South Carolina's desire for reconciliation:

But, the virtuous, are ever generous: we do not wish revenge: we earnestly wish an accommodation of our unhappy disputes with Great Britain; for, we prefer peace to war. [32]

Yet a just reconciliation appeared beyond hope:

I think it my duty to declare in the awful seat of justice and before Almighty God . . . that true reconcilement never can exist between Great Britain and America, the latter being in subjection to the former.—The Almighty created America to be independent of Britain. [34]

It is clear that the first state to declare its independence (by forming an independent government) did so because Britain had abdicated government in South Carolina. As a result, South Carolina was *legally* justified in establishing an independent government. Furthermore, the leaders still desired reconciliation, but the Prohibitory Act made further attempts to gain a just reconciliation futile. Note that it was South Carolina that first acknowledged the separation and not Massachusetts (which had been the scene of British violations). South Carolina began the formation of its government with a statement that all connections with England had been severed by the Crown. The actions of the colonial leaders throughout the colonies as in South Carolina were not only necessary but also legal.

V

Neglect of the Prohibitory Act

Most history texts do not even mention the Prohibitory Act, and few deal with its significance. Why? Perhaps proper treatment of the Act seriously weakens the humanist premise that revolutions are a necessary step in human progress. Writers of textbooks have exalted revolutionaries. They tend to falsely justify actual revolutions by presenting America's independence as the desirable result of a revolution fomented by economic frictions. Nothing could be further from the truth.

Another possible reason for such neglect of the Act is derived from our failure to understand colonial history. The colonists were meticulous about legal matters and had "staked their claims on nothing else."[1] Although the colonists were convinced that Parliament had no authority over them, they possessed written charters that required their allegiance to the King, and they would not break these written agreements even after war had started. They continued to honor the King (while resisting parliamentary interferences) until the King himself severed the relationship by declaring them out of his protection. This act by the King was the legal justification for severing all attachments to Great Britain.

Conclusions as to why the Prohibitory Act has been ignored are difficult to make. However, some observations can be made about its earlier significance.

Founding Fathers

The colonial leaders viewed the Prohibitory Act as an instrument which not only exiled them from the British Empire but also made it impossible for them to further consider reconciliation. Statements by John Adams, Thomas Jefferson, and Benjamin Franklin, in addition to statements by the Continental Congress have already been cited. Also, Samuel Adams said in reference to the Prohibitory Act that "the king has thrown us out of his protection; why should we support governments under his authority?"[2] Clearly, the colonial leaders who signed the Declaration maintained that the Prohibitory Act was the direct cause of their action.

Colonial leaders other than the Signers also recognized its significance. A noted Boston judge, Edmund Quincy (Josiah Quincy's brother and John Adams' friend), dealt with its significance in a letter to John Hancock on March 25, 1776:

> And truly I think that the member of the House of Commons, who, in a ludicrous manner, inquired at 'what time the Americans were emancipated,' might have saved himself the trouble by looking into Sir William Blackstone's Commentaries, Vol. I, p. 233, upon the duties of kings; where he would have found it to be a maxim of common law, that, when protection ceaseth, allegiance ceaseth to be the duty of the subject. Now, it being evident that the British king had, at the time of inquiry, not only withdrawn his protection from these Colonies [by his speech which proposed the Prohibitory Act] ... but that he had positively commenced hostilities, of which there can be no dubious construction.... And, if this was really the general opinion of the British Legislature [that the colonists were slaves], it is indeed full time that we should

oblige them to come to an *eclaircissement* [clarification] upon the important subject; and, at present, I can see nothing will answer the end so well AS A DECLARATION TO ALL THE WORLD OF OUR ABSOLUTE INDEPENDENCY.

Quincy concluded his letter to Hancock:

I thank you for the king's silly proclamation, in which I observe a reference to an Act made to repeal the Boston Port Bill, etc., and to empower the king's commissioners to grant the colonists pardon of their rebellious proceeding, etc., one bait of a hook ready gauged; but hope will not be a catcher of men of high or low degree.[3]

It is apparent that Quincy had learned about the Prohibitory Act from Hancock. Consequently, he wrote his son, Henry, on March 30, 1776:

I'm concerned for the British State. Her late and present impolitic measures are cutting the Cords by which Britain and America were once and lately held in Union together. The Consequences of a Separation to the Old Country I fear, but it will be *final issue* of the present Quarrel, possible not long first. I Suspect whether North America can be otherwise in tolerable Safety.[4]

Colonial Newspapers

The attention given the Prohibitory Act by colonial newspapers reflects the decided importance of the Act to the colonists. The *Boston Gazette* (March 11, 1776) printed an excerpt from a London publication dated November 13, 1775, that had viewed Lord Howe's appointment as a peace commissioner (proposed by the Prohibitory Act) as being ridiculous. It concluded, "Discerning men already say this COMMISSION SCHEME WILL NOT SUCCEED. Americans will not treat with those men ... who advised the late barbarous, bloody [war] against her."[5] Although the Prohibitory Act had not yet been passed, its effect had been accurately predicted.

Also on March 11, the *Gazette* quoted a Philadelphia publication (February 21) that indicated the colonial papers were keenly interested in the progress of the Prohibitory Act: "The bill for seizing all American property had passed the House of Lords."[6] It appears that the Americans were as yet unfamiliar with the provisions of the bill that would remove them from Britain's protection and cut them off from the Empire. Nonetheless, these reports about the Prohibitory Act were considered important enough to be printed in the same issue that proclaimed the success of the Continental Army in gaining Dorchester Heights at Boston. (This success enabled the Americans to force the British troops to evacuate Boston.)

In the March 18 issue there was a warning that peace commissioners, as authorized by the Prohibitory Act, should be sent to the Continental Congress and were not to be interviewed by individual colonies or persons.[7]

On March 25 the *Gazette* published a sermon by Peter Thacker in which he denounced Britain's pretended efforts at reconciliation in the Prohibitory Act. British acts over the past twelve years had made a just reconciliation impossible. He concluded by remarking that he thought he could hear a voice from heaven declaring, "Come out from among them and be ye separate."[8]

An editorial article in the same issue suggested that some of the general provisions of the Prohibitory Act were known by March 25. In the mind of the editor (because of the Prohibitory Act) there was no reason that independence should not be declared:

> As England has by their King's Proclamation and an act of their Parliament, not only declared war, but a piratical war against us; why should we not declare an *Independence* and use the aid of any power under heaven, to repel those pirates.[9]

Attention was given to the Prohibitory Act in the same issue that devoted a long article to the evacuation of Boston by the British troops, the most glorious event in the American colonies for the past year.

The April 1 issue of the *Gazette* published a March 16 proclamation by the Congress calling the colonists to prayer. The request was partly caused by the Prohibitory Act. Friday, May 17, was set aside as a day of *Humiliation, Fasting* and *Prayer;* that we may with united hearts confess and bewail our manifold sins and transgressions, and by a sincere repentance and amendment of life appease his righteous displeasures, and through the merits and mediation of Jesus Christ, obtain his pardon and forgiveness. Humbly imploring his assistance in frustrating the cruel purposes of our unnatural enemies; and by inclining their hearts to justice and benevolence, prevent the further effusion of kindred blood.[10]

The April 8 issue of the *Boston Gazette* reviewed a March 13 proclamation in which the Congress stated that the Prohibitory Act had forced them to continue a war of defense. The proclamation reviewed the scorn for colonial petitions, the acts of war, the agitation of the Negroes and Indians against the colonists, and then denounced the Prohibitory Act:

Whereas the Parliament of Great Britain hath lately passed an act, affirming their colonies to be in open Rebellion, forbidding all Trade and Commerce with the Inhabitants thereof, until they shall accept Pardons and submit to despotic Rule; declaring their property, wherever found upon the Water, liable to Seizure and Confiscation; and enacting that what had been done there, by Virtue of the Royal Authority were just and lawful acts and shall be so deemed.[11]

The Congress concluded that the Act was a scheme to deprive the American colonies of their liberty, a scheme to be "pertinaciously pursued," contrary to the "Laws of Nature and the English Constitution."[12]

As indicated by excerpts from the *Boston Gazette,* colonial newspapers followed the development and consequences of the Prohibitory Act with interest. The editor of the *Gazette,* like other colonial leaders, saw that the Prohibitory Act offered no basis for a genuine reconciliation (which had been promised), but that it instead authorized a war of conquest against the American colonies.

Early Historians

The Founding Fathers placed utmost significance upon the Prohibitory Act. In addition, historians contemporary with the Fathers, like Mercy Warren and David Ramsay (who have already been cited), also asserted that the act absolved the colonists of allegiance to the King.

The famous nineteenth-century historian, George Bancroft, acknowledges that the Act forced the colonists out of the Empire and made reconciliation impossible, but he failed to show that the Prohibitory Act made the colonists independent of the King:

American statesmen had struggled to avoid a separation; the measures of the British government, as one by one they were necessarily borne across the Atlantic—disregard of the petition [Olive Branch] of Congress by the king, his speech to Parliament, his avowed negotiations for mercenaries, the closure of the ports of all the thirteen colonies and the confiscation of all their property on the ocean [Prohibitory Act]—forced upon them the conviction that they must protect and govern themselves.[13]

Bancroft also notes the significance of the Prohibitory Act in relation to the proposal for independence made by the Congress in May of 1776:

Recalling the act of parliament which excluded the Americans from the protection of the crown, the king's neglect to return any answer whatever to their petition ... they declared that it was "absolutely irreconcilable with reason and good conscience for the people of these colonies now to take the oaths and affirmations necessary for the support of any government under the crown of Great Britain."[14]

The Prohibitory Act had some very particular effects: for example, according to Emma Willard, the Act caused the colonial flag to be changed. Although the colonies used many different flags, there had been a growing unanimity for a red flag (at that time a red flag was symbolic of defensive warfare). Willard says that "such indignant feelings were excited, that their flag which had hitherto been plain red, was changed to thirteen stripes, as emblematical of the union of the colonies."[15] Although Willard does not deal with its legal significance, she does suggest that the Prohibitory Act was the focal point of American independence.

Twentieth-Century Historians

Historians of the early twentieth century placed varying emphasis upon the Act. Elroy McKendree Avery in his multi-volumed history briefly discussed how the King's speech of October 26 forced the colonists into independence, but did not mention the Act.[16]

A history by Sydney George Fisher (published in 1908) presents the colonial viewpoint:

> The situation had been made still more favorable for the patriots by the passage in Parliament of a new bill, which became law on the 21st of December, 1775, and was known as the Prohibitory Act. It was intended by the Ministry to meet the increasing difficulties of the situation, and establish a legal and legislative basis for the coercion and subjugation of the colonies.[17]

Fisher outlines the provisions of the Act and then states:

> The Ministry had, of course, thought that it was necessary to pass some such act legalizing the warfare which was to be waged against the colonies and notifying all nations that a state of war existed ... Parliament and the King by thus declaring war upon the colonies were voluntarily giving them the legal status of a foreign nation, and declaring them independent. If war had to be formally declared against them they must be already independent, and were not rebels.[18]

Fisher refers to the King's speech and to Parliament's assent to the King. He emphasizes the significance of the Act:

> Protection and allegiance were reciprocal. There could be no allegiance where there was no protection. The allegiance to the King had been given in exchange for his protection; and when his protection was withdrawn by a declaration of war, the allegiance was annulled.[19]

Fisher believed that there were hundreds of undecided who were willing to discuss independence after the passage of the Act but who had been unwilling before:

The argument was so common the year before that America was waging war merely for the sake of returning to the old semi-independent condition that prevailed the year 1763, was now abandoned.[20]

He cites an example of the personal conflict experienced by many colonists until they learned of the Prohibitory Act:

Elias Boudinot tells us that, having at one time as a colonial official taken the British oath of allegiance, he hardly knew what course to pursue in the Revolution until the Prohibitory Act relieved him of all scruples of conscience. Doubtless there were hundreds of others who, seeing protection and allegiance destroyed by act of Parliament, reasoned that there could be no binding oath to support an allegiance which no longer existed.[21]

Between the world wars, progressive historians (Carl Becker, Charles Beard, and Arthur Schlesinger) presented the "Revolution" in the modern sense, as a revolution that established a collective democracy. This view gathered wide acceptance. However, their confidence in the essential goodness of collective democracies was so shaken by the rise of Hitler, Mussolini, and Stalin that Becker, Beard, and Schlesinger radically altered their presentations of the "Revolution."

Since the Second World War, Becker has emphasized the fact that the colonists did not want independence and that the Prohibitory Act forced it upon them:

The hope of reconciliation died slowly. Even after the king refused to receive the Petition, even after the British Government issued the Prohibitory Act, December 22, 1775 . . . many men still clung to this hope. They clung to it in desperation, partly because they had so often and so explicitly declared that separation was no part of their purpose and utterly abhorrent to their desire. . . They had long been proud of the British empire, of its achievements, of its name and fame in the world; it was their empire too . . . Not desire, but practical difficulties, forced them to adopt separation from Great Britain as the object of their efforts. In the winter of 1776 the trend of opinion was towards independence as the only alternative to submission.[22]

Robert E. Brown, in particular, discusses the recantation of these progressive historians and writes that most recent historians no longer support the idea that the American "Revolution" was a revolution in the modern sense. He makes the following conclusion:

"Did the American Revolution really happen?" My answer is yes and no. Yes, if we mean that it involved a change in American attitude toward the British, that it began in 1761 (or earlier) and ended in 1776, and that it was a movement to preserve a democratic society from the encroachments of British Imperialism.[23]

Brown denies that the "Revolution" involved class warfare or that it democratized America. He also denies that the Declaration, the state constitutions, and the Articles were instruments intended to establish a collective democracy "only to be thwarted in the end by the adoption of a counter-revolutionary Constitution." He agrees with de Tocqueville that America "had never experienced a class revolution because it had never needed one." He then summarizes, "The late conversion of Becker, Beard, and Schlesinger demonstrates what happens when scholars forget their functions . . . Good causes do not need false prophets."[24]

Also in this inter-war period, the neglect of the Prohibitory Act began. Although recent historians do not accept the progressive view and even though some progressives have changed their ideas on the "Revolution," the neglect of the Prohibitory Act has continued.

A look at several dozen United States history texts published since World War II reveals that only about one in ten even mentions the Prohibitory Act. The following list is only a sampling of those texts surveyed (college and high school) which fail to mention it:

Bailey, Thomas A., and Kennedy, David M., *The American Pageant.* Lexington, Massachusetts: D.C. Heath and Company, 1979.

Blum, John M.; Morgan, Edmund S.; Rose, Willie Lee; Schlesinger, Arthur M., Jr.; Stampp, Kenneth M.; and Woodward, C. Vann. *The National Experience.* New York: Harcourt, Brace, Jovanovich, Inc., 1977.

Boyle, Donzella Cross. *Quest of a Hemisphere*. Boston: Western Islands, 1970.

Canfield, Leon H., and Wilder, Howard B. *The Making of Modern America*. Boston: Houghton Mifflin Company, 1962.
Page 100 of this text refers to "an act of Parliament that prohibited all trade and other dealings with the colonies" but does not mention the Prohibitory Act by name.

Carman, Harry J.; Syrett, Harold C.; and Wishy, Bernard W. *A History of the American People*. New York: Alfred A. Knopf, 1960.

Chase, John Terry. *The Study of American History*. Guilford, Connecticut: Duskin Publishing Group, Inc., 1974.
This text refers to the King's proclamation of October 26, 1775, on page 157, but does not mention the Prohibitory Act.

Clark, James I., and Remini, Robert V. *We the People*. Beverly Hills: Glencoe Press, 1975.

Dollar, Charles M.; Gunderson, Joan Rezner; Satz, Ronald N.; Nelson, H. Viscount, Jr.; and Reichard, Gary. *America: Changing Times*. New York: John Wiley and Sons, 1979.

Faulkner, Harold Underwood. *American Political and Social History*. New York: Appleton-Century-Crofts, Inc., 1957.

Garraty, John A. *The American Nation*. New York: Harper and Row, 1979.

Graff, Henry F. *The Free and the Brave*. Chicago: Rand McNally and Company, 1967.

Gruver, Rebecca Brooks. *An American History*. Reading, Massachusetts: Addison-Wesley Publishing Company, 1976.

Ingle, H. L., and Ward, James A. *American History: A Brief View*. Boston: Little, Brown and Company, 1978.

Muzzey, David Saville. *Our Country's History*. Boston: Ginn and Company, 1957.

Riegel, Robert E., and Athearn, Robert G. *America Moves West*. New York: Holt, Rinehart, and Winston, Inc., 1971.

Unger, Irwin. *These United States: The Questions of Our Past*. Boston: Little, Brown, and Company, 1978.

Weinstein, Allen, and Wilson, R. Jackson. *An American History: Freedom and Crisis*. New York: Random House, Inc., 1974.

Weisberger, Bernard A. *Pathways to the Present*. New York: Harper and Row, 1976.

Wood, Leonard C.; Gabriel, Ralph H.; and Biller, Edward L. *America: Its People and Values*. New York: Harcourt, Brace, Jovanovich, Inc., 1975.

The percentage of books that mention the Prohibitory Act increases when works that concentrate specifically on the "Revolution" and colonial period are included. Still, the majority do not deal with the Act. It is particularly surprising that books like *The Reinterpretation of the American Revolution,* edited by Jack P. Greene, do not refer to it. This book has contributions by over a dozen historians who specialize in the Revolutionary Period: Curtis P. Nettels, Jack P. Greene, Richard Buel, Jr., Edmund S. Morgan, David S. Lovejoy, Bernard Bailyn, Perry Miller, Cecilia M. Kenyon, Jackson Turner Main, R. R. Palmer, Forrest McDonald, Douglas G. Adair, J. R. Pole, John P. Roche, Arthur O. Lovejoy, Martin Diamond, and Hannah Arendt. There are 29 specific references to the Stamp Act, but none to the Prohibitory Act.

Other works that concentrate in the period, but do not mention the Act are as follows:

Hall, Verna M. *The Christian History of the American Revolution: Consider and Ponder*. San Francisco: Foundations of American Christian Education, 1976.

Maier, Pauline. *From Resistance to Revolution*. New York: Alfred A. Knopf, 1972.

Noll, Mark A. *Christians in the American Revolution*. Washington: Christian University Press, 1977.

Rossiter, Clinton. *Seedtime of the Republic*. New York: Harcourt, Brace and Company, 1953.

Winsor, Justin., ed. *The American Revolution*. New York: Bicentennial Sons of Liberty Publication, Land's End Press, 1972.
This extensive work on the Revolution holds George III responsible for the separation, but does not mention the Prohibitory Act: "As we have seen it was the royal scorn of that petition, backed by a willful personal espousal of responsibility, which made the king the real prompter of the Declaration of Independence" (p. 249).

One survey text mentions the Act, but attaches little significance to it: "In the Prohibitory Act of December 1775, Parliament barred all trade with the rebellious colonies and ordered their ships confiscated." It then refers to news about the hiring of mercenaries being received at the same time but makes no further reference to the Act.[25]

Several works that deal with the "Revolution" take the position that the Prohibitory Act forced independence upon the colonists, but do not mention that the king removed his protection. John Richard Alden in *The American Revolution, 1775-1783* says:

On November 20, 1775, North brought before the Commons a Prohibitory Bill which passed into law in similar fashion ... In effect, both King and Parliament had now given their answer to the Olive Branch Petition—Britain would wage war with all the strength at her command. Their reply could have only one result—to force hundreds of thousands of Americans who had wished for no more than what they considered their rights within the empire to take the road to independence.[26]

This work goes on to say:

... it was normal practice to employ mercenaries against foreign enemies, but the hiring of them by Britain seemed irrefutable proof to the colonists that they were to be treated as foreigners.[27]

David Hawke in *The Colonial Experience* states:

... on February 27 Congress received a copy of the Prohibitory Act, which had passed Parliament on

December 22, 1775. The act gave statutory force to the ministry's program and made clear that all branches of the British government were united in coercing the colonies into submission... Moderates were stunned by the measure. "Nothing is left now but to fight it out," said Joseph Hewes of North Carolina. An "Act of Independency," John Adams called it, "for the King Lords and Commons have united in sundering this country from that I think forever."[28]

Hawke, by not giving Adam's complete statement, failed to show that the Prohibitory Act removed protection from the thirteen colonies. Adam's complete comments regarding the Act are as follows:

I know not whether you have seen the Act of Parliament called the restraining Act, or prohibitory Act, or piratical Act, or plundering Act, or Act of Independency, for by all of these titles is it called. I think the most apposite is the Act of Independency, for King Lords and Commons have united in sundering this country from that I think forever. It is a compleat Dismemberment of the British Empire. It throws thirteen colonies out of the Royal Protection, levels all distinctions, and makes us independent in spight of our supplications and entreaties.[29]

Curtis P. Nettels in *The Roots of American Civilization* states:

In August, George III refused to receive the Olive Branch Petition ... and on August 23 he issued a proclamation stigmatizing the Americans as rebels and ordering that all persons refrain from giving them assistance. Parliament completed the work of repression by an act of December 22, 1775, which prohibited all trade with the thirteen colonies—an act embodying the view of Lord North that because 'the Americans had refused to trade with Great Britain, it was but just that they be not suffered to trade with any other nation.'[30]

Nettels goes on to suggest that the Prohibitory Act forced the colonists to declare their independence, but neglects to mention that the King removed the colonists from his protection and thus made them independent.

Marshall Smelser in *The Winning of Independence* says:

> In November Parliament responded with the Prohibitory Act to blockade America .... In pacification the government promised to send commissioners to America to absolve the contrite. Many Americans read the Prohibitory Act as expulsion from the Empire.[31]
> What most strengthened the cause of independence was the painful mental impact of the Prohibitory Act, which was as important to independence as the Boston Port Act has been to contumacy. Such an excommunication technically banned colonial trade entirely, and closed off North America like a hermit kingdom.[32]
> The quarantine of the colonies by act of Parliament, which closed the colonies to all commerce and is usually called the Prohibitory Act ... was known in America late in February 1776. This act was little short of a process of outlawry and could be interpreted as Parliament's declaration of American Independence.[33]

Both Smelser and Weldon A. Brown emphasize the Act, but fail to discuss the removal of protection.[34]

Current, Williams, and Friedel in *American History: A Survey* treat the subject in a similar fashion:

> And, most important, they felt that they were being forced into independence when the British government replied to the Olive Branch Petition with the Prohibitory Act... The Americans desperately needed military supplies to continue the war, and now they could get them from abroad in adequate amounts only if they broke completely with Great Britain and proceeded to behave in all respects as if they comprised a sovereign nation.[35]

A few works suggest that the Prohibitory Act made the colonies legally independent, but they do not explain why.

Henry Steele Commager and Richard B. Morris in *The Spirit of 'Seventy-Six'* state:

> But as the royal program made its inexorable progress through Parliament, the worst forebodings of the opposition were realized, one by one. The Americans were treated as unruly children; they were punished; they were excluded from trade and from the fisheries; they

were finally pronounced rebels and *ousted from the empire even before they had ousted themselves!* By these steps Lord North and his royal master proved that the quarrel was not subject to rational solution.[36]

Surprisingly, Commager's *Documents of American History* does not contain a single reference to the Prohibitory Act.[37]

A work published during World War II acknowledges that the Act removed protection, but does not discuss the legal significance of that removal. Edmund Cody Burnett in *The Continental Congress* states:

> And the British government itself was not the least of these contributing factors; for, by an act of Parliament December 22, 1775, the colonies were removed from the protection of the crown, trade with them prohibited and seizure and confiscation of American ships at sea authorized. It was the last days of February that an advance copy of the act came by surreptitious means under the eyes of Congress and its effect was to propel the colonies violently toward independence.[38]

Only a few works since World War II have dealt with the significance of the removal of protection (and then only briefly).

Cornelia Meigs in *The Violent Men* sympathetically presents the men in the First and Second Continental Congresses as men who preferred to forsake self-interests rather than to jeopardize liberty. She closely examines the petitions and their rejections, but does not mention the King's speech or the Prohibitory Act by name. She acknowledges that "things had changed in the course of a month"[39] (February 1776), but she does not mention the Prohibitory Act as the cause of that change. She presents the argument of those who favored independence:

> Why talk of minds becoming accommodated when the fact was already established? England had cut off the colonies from her protection, had forbidden all commercial intercourse with them, had decreed that their property was forfeit, that every ship taken at sea was a lawful prize. Was there anything left of dependence in all this? Here was actual independence—why not recognize it?[40]

Scheer and Rankin in *Rebels and Redcoats* comment:

> The passage by Parliament of the Prohibitory Act at the end of 1775, notifying all nations that a state of war existed, delighted the more radical Whigs; by thus declaring war, England voluntarily gave the colonies the legal status of a foreign nation—and therefore an independent one. By removing his protection, they reasoned, the King forfeited the colonies [sic] allegiance. Hundreds of Americans were relieved of the disagreeable decision for independence. In a sense, it was thrust upon them, and talk of independence, previously upon the tongues of the radicals only, became common.[41]

Thomas Fleming in *1776: Year of Illusions* makes several references to the Prohibitory Act, but always lets his "characters" tell the reason for the Separation. He does not stress the importance of the Act except in its commercial sense.[42]

It is possible to examine dozens of American history encyclopedias (even those dealing specifically with the American "Revolution") without finding a single entry for the Prohibitory Act. This neglect exists in spite of the fact that the colonists saw it as the measure that removed them from the British Empire.

It is impossible at this point to establish definite patterns in the neglect of the Prohibitory Act. However, tendencies do appear. The patriot contemporaries certainly emphasized that the Act absolved the colonists of allegiance. It also appears that this emphasis was generally maintained by American historians through the nineteenth century and into the twentieth. Furthermore, there are indications that the Act's significance began to be neglected between World War I and World War II. (The advent of a progressive interpretation of the "Revolution" is certainly a factor in this neglect.) Since World War II, historians, for the most part, have neglected the Prohibitory Act. Few deal with the legal consequence of the removal of the King's protection, although some have recognized that it forced independence upon the colonists.

In recent years, historians of the "Revolution" have, on the whole, returned to presenting the "Revolution" as a just defense of freedoms rather than as a revolutionary overthrow by discontented colonists. Nonetheless, a return to presenting the Prohibitory Act as a removal of the colonists' legal obligation to the King (the only allegiance which they had ever recognized) cannot be discerned.

VI

Conclusion

Not a Revolution

Historians acknowledge that colonial religious and political leaders did not talk, look, nor act like revolutionaries. They also acknowledge that the American "Revolution" did not have the consequences of a modern revolution. According to many historians, the colonial leaders sacrificially maintained a new order and gained the respect of their contemporaries and their posterity.

Robert E. Brown says: "In Massachusetts . . . we find one of the unique 'revolutions' in world history—a revolution to preserve a social order rather than to change it."[1] Carl N. Degler concludes that the colonial leaders "were a strange new breed—contented revolutionaries."[2] Neil R. Stout points out that "the twenty-seven delegates to the Stamp Act Congress were anything but radical; nevertheless, they clearly stated the constitutional case against Parliament's taxing America."[3] These historians concede that there was no revolution. The colonists did not desire change but preservation. Jesse Lemisch says in this regard: "to explain it [the Separation] as the result of efficient propaganda is to belittle the reality of the grievance and to suggest that the Americans were largely content until they were aroused by a few demagogues."[4] Gordon S. Wood: "The issue then ... was no more and no less than separation from Britain and the *preservation of American liberty.*"[5]

Further, the Separation did not have the results of an actual revolution. Irving Kristol observes that "this was a revolution which, unlike all subsequent revolutions, did not devour its children: the men who made the revolution were the men who went on to create the new political order, who then held the highest elective positions in the order, and who all died in bed."[6] In an attempt to explain the "Revolution," Kristol continues: "a successful revolution is best accomplished by a people who do not really want it at all, but find themselves reluctantly making it. The American Revolution was exactly such a reluctant revolution."[7] In fact, it could be argued that there was no revolution at all.

The Separation from Britain has been misnamed a revolution partly because the colonists called it a revolution. But the term has changed meanings. Today the word "revolution" is defined in *Webster's New Collegiate Dictionary* as "a fundamental change in political organizations; esp: the overthrow or renunciation of one government or ruler and the substitution of another by the governed." As the word is commonly used today, it refers to a violent overthrow of government.

In the original edition of *Webster's Dictionary* (1828), the definition is something quite different: "6. In *politics,* a material or entire change in the constitution of government. Thus the revolution in England, in 1688, was produced by the abdication of King James II, the establishment of the house of Orange upon the throne, and the restoration of the constitution to its primitive state." The next definition is simply; "7. Motion backward." The term "revolution" as used then implied a return to formerly held principles.

Further evidence that, to colonial Americans, the term implied a just and necessary resistance is found in statements by their contemporaries in England. For example, John Wilkes (Member of Parliament) stated that "A fit and proper resistance . . . is a revolution, not a rebellion."[8]

Because *revolution* was the proper term to express what they had accomplished, the colonists used it consistently. However, it is confusing to modern Americans who have acquired a modern concept of a violent, guerrilla-styled overthrow. Understanding the change in meaning helps one to understand why the colonists consistently referred to their resistance as a *revolution* and why the British government persisted in calling it a *rebellion*.

In the opinion of the colonists they had not resisted lawful authority, but had exhausted every possible peaceful means of obtaining justice. Therefore, they were not ashamed but proud. They were proud to preserve a system of written laws rather than to submit to an unwritten constitution executed by a capricious King and Parliament. The substitution of *royal* authority had been forced upon them by the King and Parliament through the Prohibitory Act. It was Britain, not the colonies, that had attempted a radical change.

The word "revolution" was used to describe the defense of a free society that had matured for 150 years. These people maintained their freedom in spite of unconstituted and authoritarian powers in England that had become increasingly hostile since 1763. The continued preservation of their institutions (for which they had left the Old World and come to the New) was at stake. It was therefore an "English Revolution," not an "American Revolution."

Another source of confusion was that the Americans had become increasingly unlike the English. Differences began to appear in the churches, governments, culture, moral attitudes, and economic policies of the American colonies for generations before the war with Britain. But this process was not a revolution.

An examination of this so-called "Revolution" reveals a lack of military strategy, dedicated leadership, united authority, and general preparedness. There was no formal government, no formal declaration of war, no crystalized intent. The military action was initially only an attempt to remove the British troops and to keep them from enforcing the "repressive and illegal Parliamentary acts." The colonists considered it a defensive action to protect their rights which they believed were guaranteed by the British Constitution. Brilliant and distinguished British legalists like Chatham, Burke, and Fox viewed the American colonist as the champion of English liberties.

The colonists had not wanted separation in the early stages. They were blessed of God as no other people, in or out of the British Empire. A prosperous people do not make anarchists, especially when they realize that their blessings have been given to them through God's instrument: orderly government. The colonists resisted in self-discipline. They wanted redress, not rebellion or war. The participants in the eventual Separation expressed enthusiasm, tempered with an anxious examination of their goals.

No comparatively large armies were involved on either side. There was little mob violence, and even the military engagements were remarkably mild and bloodless. Although there were cruelties, both sides generally observed the rules of eighteenth-century warfare. There was no savagery. The colonists produced no literature of disillusionment and made no bold promises. Anarchy was denounced, not encouraged. When it was over, there were no military tribunals, no reigns of terror. The leaders were prosperous, conservative, and benevolent. They abhorred fanaticism and lawlessness. They were not revolutionaries and did not promote a revolution.

Independence Not Sought

God apparently used two contradictory assumptions to achieve independence for the colonists. The English government assumed that the colonists had from the beginning wanted nothing but independence. Colonial leaders, on the other hand, assumed that England's policy after 1763 was to force an absolute and unconditional submission upon the colonists. The military struggle began and ended with both sides retaining these beliefs.

Independence from Britain did not produce a more democratic way of life—the colonists had already had one. It did not establish new institutions; it preserved existing ones. The colonists were defenders and conservationists, not rebels. They had desired only a restoration of the Empire as it had existed before 1763, not independence.

God Aided American Independence

Placed in proper perspective, the Prohibitory Act of December 22, 1775, may have accomplished through George III and Parliament what most of the colonists asserted they did not want: independence. Did God use this Act to give the colonists what they apparently would not have sought and secured for themselves?

American independence has certainly served the purpose and plan of God. All of God's purpose cannot be known, but it is clear that American liberties have resulted in religious freedom and prosperity for millions.

Further Considerations

The American "Revolution" still fascinates both historians and students of history as they seek to determine causes for the events of those two fateful decades—1763-1783. The conclusions of historians vary. On one extreme, Charles A. Beard sees the Founders' motives for Separation as purely economic.[9] On the opposite extreme, George Bancroft presents the Separation as a great patriotic struggle for liberty.[10] Between these two views are many other interpretations: the "Revolution" was a legal dispute, a resistance to a conspired tyranny against the colonies, or an act of colonial disloyalty to the mother nation. It has been viewed as the result of a long-smouldering desire for independence; an outmoded system of mercantilism; economic conflicts within the Empire; social and class movements; a struggle between the intellectuals and aristocrats; the blunders of George III and his supporters; and many other social, political, and economic problems.

Perhaps Perry Miller used the right approach with his thesis that the "Revolution" came as a result of the disobedience of the people of this nation in failing to continue the spiritual emphasis of the Great Awakening. Many believed the necessity to defend life and home was the inevitable result of disobedience to God. God was punishing his people.[11]

The timing of the military and political success of the Separation indicates something more than coincidence. Shortly after the Prohibitory Act was passed, England was fighting a real war on the continent. France, Spain, Holland, Ireland, Russia, Denmark, Norway, Sweden, the "Holy Roman Empire" (Germany), Prussia, and Portugal all fought against Great Britain. She was forced to fight the American colonies with hired mercenaries while keeping her best military personnel in Europe. England deliberately, but reluctantly, admitted defeat to the Americans in order to save her resources for the real war on the continent. God made the war in the colonies decidedly secondary to England's main concern.

The best evidence of God's dealing with America may be seen in the peace treaty of 1783. It was the most generous treaty that history records—even though the American colonies had not won a conclusive victory. Out of all the nations allied in war against Britain, only the United States gained significant concessions. God gave independence and a large territory to the American colonists—a priceless birthright and heritage. They were to be the stewards of both freedom and property. Such blessings demanded obedience to God's Word.

The American colonists were, on the whole, a people who honored God and His Word. They had resisted authoritarian attempts by Great Britain to change their colonial relationship because they feared tyranny. Colonial leaders feared religious tyranny most because it would jeopardize their liberty to obey God's Word. It seems that God rewarded their reverence of His Word by aiding their resistance to Britain and their separation from Britain. Because of God's evident blessings upon the thirteen colonies, many colonial clergymen claimed for America the promise given to Israel in Deuteronomy 26:15-19:

15 Look down from thy holy habitation, from heaven, and bless thy people Israel, and the land which thou hast given us, as thou swarest unto our fathers, a land that floweth with milk and honey.

16 This day the Lord thy God hath commanded thee to do these statutes and judgments: thou shalt therefore keep and do them with all thine heart, and with all thy soul.

17 Thou hast avouched the Lord this day to be thy God, and to walk in his ways, and to keep his statutes, and his commandments, and his judgments, and to hearken unto his voice:

18 And the Lord hath avouched thee this day to be his peculiar people, as he hath promised thee, and that thou shouldest keep all his commandments;

19 And to make thee high above all nations which he hath made, in praise, and in name, and in honour; and that thou mayest be an holy people unto the Lord thy God, as he hath spoken.

Documents

Several documents are related to American independence, and some of the more important ones are printed here for the reader's convenience. In addition, an abridgment of the Prohibitory Act has been included. Those sections from which excerpts have been quoted in this work are printed in their entirety. Only those sections that deal primarily with the technical aspects of enforcement have been abridged.

English Bill of Rights

The declaration of rights presented by the Lords and Commons to William and Mary on February 13, 1689, was formally enacted into law on December 16, 1689.

WHEREAS the late King *James* the Second, by the assistance of divers evil counsellors, judges, and ministers employed by him, did endeavor to subvert and extirpate the protestant religion, and the laws and liberties of this kingdom.

1. By assuming and exercising a power of dispensing with and suspending of laws, and the execution of laws, without consent of parliament.

2. By committing and prosecuting divers worthy prelates, for humbly petitioning to be excused from concurring to the said assumed power.

3. By issuing and causing to be executed a commission under the great seal for erecting a court called, *The court of commissioners for ecclesiastical causes.*

4. By levying money for and to the use of the crown, by pretence of prerogative, for other time, and in other manner, than the same was granted by parliament.

5. By raising and keeping a standing army within this kingdom in time of peace, without consent of parliament, and quartering soldiers contrary to law.

6. By causing several good subjects, being protestants, to be disarmed, at the same time when papists were both armed and employed, contrary to law.

7. By violating the freedom of election of members to serve in parliament.

8. By prosecutions in the court of King's bench, for matters and causes cognizable only in parliament; and by divers other arbitrary and illegal courses.

9. And whereas of late years, partial, corrupt, and unqualified persons have been returned and served on juries in trials, and particularly divers jurors in trials for high treason, which were not freeholders.

10. And excessive bail hath been required of persons committed in criminal cases, to elude the benefit of the laws made for the liberty of the subjects.

11. And excessive fines have been imposed; and illegal and cruel punishments have been inflicted.

12. And several grants and promises made of fines and forfeitures, before any conviction or judgment against the persons, upon whom the same were to be levied.

All which are utterly and directly contrary to the known laws and statutes, and freedom of this realm.

And whereas the said late king *James* the Second having abdicated the government, and the throne being thereby vacant . . . the said lords spiritual and temporal, and commons . . . do in the first place (as their ancestors in like case have usually done) for the vindicating and asserting their ancient rights and liberties, declare;

1. That the pretended power of suspending of laws, or the execution of laws, by regal authority, without consent of parliament, is illegal.

2. That the pretended power of dispensing with laws, or the execution of laws, by regal authority, as it hath been assumed and exercised of late, is illegal.

3. That the commission for erecting the late court of commissioners for ecclesiastical causes, and all other commissions and courts of like nature are illegal and pernicious.

4. That levying money for or to the use of the crown, by pretence of prerogative, without grant of parliament, for longer time, or in other manner than the same is or shall be granted, is illegal.

5. That it is the right of the subjects to petition the King, and all committments and prosecutions for such petitioning are illegal.

6. That the raising or keeping a standing army within the kingdom in time of peace, unless it be with consent of parliament, is against law.

7. That the subjects which are protestants, may have arms for their defence suitable to their conditions, and as allowed by law.

8. That election of members of parliament ought to be free.

9. That the freedom of speech, and debates or proceedings in parliament, ought not to be impeached or questioned in any court or place out of parliament.

10. That excessive bail ought not to be required, nor excessive fines imposed; nor cruel and unusual punishments

inflicted.

11. That jurors ought to be duly impanelled and returned, and jurors which pass upon men in trials for high treason ought to be freeholders.

12. That all grants and promises of fines and forfeitures of particular persons before conviction, are illegal and void.

13. And that for redress of all grievances, and for the amending, strengthening, and preserving of the laws, parliaments ought to be held frequently.

And they do claim, demand, and insist upon all and singular the premisses, as their undoubted rights and liberties; and that no declarations, judgments, doings or proceedings, to the prejudice of the people in any of the said premisses, ought in any wise to be drawn hereafter into consequence or example.

Petition to the King
(Approved by the Continental Congress on October 25, 1774)
To the Kings Most Excellent Majesty.
Most Gracious Sovereign,

We your majestys faithful subjects of the colonies of Newhampshire, Massachusetts-bay, Rhode-island and Providence Plantations, Connecticut, New-York, New-Jersey, Pennsylvania, the counties of New-Castle Kent and Sussex on Delaware, Maryland, Virginia, North Carolina, and South Carolina, in behalf of ourselves and the inhabitants of these colonies who have deputed us to represent them in General Congress, by this our humble petition, beg leave to lay our grievances before the throne.

A standing army has been kept in these colonies, ever since the conclusion of the late war, without the consent of our assemblies; and this army with a considerable naval armament has been employed to enforce the collection of taxes.

The Authority of the commander in chief, and, under him, of the brigadiers general has in time of peace, been rendered supreme in all the civil governments in America.

The commander in chief of all your majesty's forces in North-America has, in time of peace, been appointed governor of a colony.

The charges of usual offices have been greatly increased; and, new, expensive and oppressive offices have been multiplied.

The judges of admiralty and vice-admiralty courts are empowered to receive their salaries and fees from the effects condemned by themselves. The officers of the customs are empowered to break open and enter houses without the authority of any civil magistrate founded on legal information.

The judges of courts of common law have been made entirely dependent on one part of the legislature for their salaries, as well as for the duration of their commissions.

Councellors holding their commissions, during pleasure, exercise legislative authority.

Humble and reasonable petitions from the representatives of the people have been fruitless.

The agents of the people have been discountenanced and governors have been instructed to prevent the payment of their salaries.

Assemblies have been repeatedly and injuriously dissolved.

Commerce has been burthened with many useless and oppressive restrictions.

By several acts of parliament made in the fourth, fifth, sixth, seventh, and eighth years of your majesty's reign, duties are imposed on us, for the purpose of raising a revenue, and the powers of admiralty and vice-admiralty courts are extended beyond their ancient limits, whereby our property is taken from us without our consent, the trial by jury in many civil cases is abolished, enormous forfeitures are incurred for slight offences, vexatious informers are exempted from paying damages, to which they are justly liable, and oppressive security is required from owners before they are allowed to defend their right.

Both houses of parliament have resolved that colonists may be tried in England, for offences alleged to have been committed in America, by virtue of a statute passed in the thirty fifth year of Henry the eighth; and in consequence thereof, attempts have been made to enforce that statute. A statute was passed in the twelfth year of your majesty's reign, directing, that persons charged with committing any offence therein described, in any place out of the realm, may be indicted and tried for the same, in any shire or county within the realm, whereby inhabitants of these colonies may, in sundry cases by that statute made capital, be deprived of a trial by their peers of the vicinage.

In the last sessions of the parliament, an act was passed for blocking up the harbour of Boston; another, empowering the governor of the Massachussets-bay to send persons indicted for murder in that province to another colony or even to Great Britain for trial whereby such offenders may escape legal punishment; a third, for altering the chartered constitution of government in that province; and a fourth for extending the limits of Quebec, abolishing the English and restoring the French laws, whereby great numbers of British freemen are subjected to the latter, and establishing an absolute government and the Roman Catholick religion throughout those vast regions, that border on the westerly and northerly boundaries of the free protestant English settlements; and a fifth for the better providing suitable quarters for officers and soldiers in his majesty's service in North-America.

To a sovereign, who "glories in the name of Briton" the bare recital of these acts must we presume, justify the loyal subjects, who fly to the foot of his throne and implore his clemency for protection against them.

From this destructive system of colony administration adopted since the conclusion of the last war, have flowed those distresses, dangers, fears and jealousies, that overwhelm your majesty's dutiful colonists with affliction; and we defy our most subtle and inveterate enemies, to trace the unhappy differences between Great-Britain and these colonies, from an earlier period or from other causes than we have assigned. Had they proceeded on our part from a restless levity of temper, unjust impulses of ambition, or artful suggestions of seditious persons, we should merit the opprobrious terms frequently bestowed upon us, by those we revere. But so far from promoting innovations, we have only opposed them; and can be charged with no offence, unless it be one, to receive injuries and be sensible of them.

Had our creator been pleased to give us existence in a land of slavery, the sense of our condition might have been mitigated by ignorance and habit. But thanks be to his adoreable goodness, we were born the heirs of freedom, and ever enjoyed our right under the auspices of your royal ancestors, whose family was seated on the British throne, to rescue and secure a pious and gallant nation from the popery and despotism of a superstitious and inexorable tyrant. Your majesty, we are confident, justly rejoices, that your title to the crown is thus founded on the title of your people to liberty; and therefore we doubt not, but your royal wisdom must approve the sensibility, that teaches your subjects anxiously to guard the blessings, they received from divine providence, and thereby to prove the performance of that compact, which elevated the illustrious house of Brunswick to the imperial dignity it now possesses.

The apprehension of being degraded into a state of

servitude from the pre-eminent rank of English free-men, while our minds retain the strongest love of liberty, and clearly foresee the miseries preparing for us and our posterity, excites emotions in our breasts, which though we cannot describe, we should not wish to conceal. Feeling as men, and thinking as subjects, in the manner we do, silence would be disloyalty. By giving this faithful information, we do all in our power, to promote the great objects of your royal cares, the tranquility of your government, and the welfare of your people.

Duty to your majesty and regard for the preservation of ourselves and our posterity, the primary obligations of nature and society command us to entreat your royal attention; and as your majesty enjoys the signal distinction of reigning over freemen, we apprehend the language of freemen can not be displeasing. Your royal indignation, we hope, will rather fall on those designing and dangerous men, who daringly interposing themselves between your royal person and your faithful subjects, and for several years past incessantly employed to dissolve the bonds of society, by abusing your majesty's authority, misrepresenting your American subjects and prosecuting the most desperate and irritating projects of oppression, have at length compelled us, by the force of accumulated injuries too severe to be any longer tolerable, to disturb your majesty's repose by our complaints.

These sentiments are extorted from hearts, that much more willingly would bleed in your majesty's service. Yet so greatly have we been misrepresented, that a necessity has been alledged of taking our property from us without our consent "to defray the charge of the administration of justice, the support of civil government, and the defence protection and security of the colonies." But we beg leave to assure your majesty, that such provision has been and will be made for defraying the two first articles, as has been and shall be judged, by the legislatures of the several colonies, just and suitable to their respective circumstances: And for the defence protection and security of the colonies, their militias, if properly regulated, as they earnestly desire may immediately be done, would be fully sufficient, at least in times of peace; and in case of war, your faithful colonists will be ready and willing, as they ever have been when constitutionally required, to demonstrate their loyalty to your majesty, by exerting their most strenuous efforts in granting supplies and raising forces. Yielding to no British subjects, in affectionate attachment to your majesty's person, family and government, we too dearly prize the privilege of expressing that attachment by those proofs, that are honourable to the prince who receives them, and to the people who give them, ever to resign it to any body of men upon earth.

Had we been permitted to enjoy in quiet the inheritance left us by our forefathers, we should at this time have been peaceably, cheerfully and usefully employed in recommending ourselves by every testimony of devotion to your majesty, and of veneration to the state, from which we derive our origin. But though now exposed to unexpected and unnatural scenes of distress by a contention with that nation, in whose parental guidance on all important affairs we have hitherto with filial reverence constantly trusted, and therefore can derive no instruction in our present unhappy and perplexing circumstances from any former experience, yet we doubt not, the purity of our intention and the integrity of our conduct will justify us at the grand tribunal, before which all mankind must submit to judgment.

We ask but for peace, liberty, and safety. We wish not a diminution of the prerogative, nor do we solicit the grant of any new right in our favour. Your royal authority over us and our connexion with Great-Britain, we shall always carefully and zealously endeavor to support and maintain.

Filled with sentiments of duty to your majesty, and of affection to our parent state, deeply impressed by our education and strongly confirmed by our reason, and anxious to evince the sincerity of these dispositions, we present this petition only to obtain redress of grievances and relief from fears and jealousies occasioned by the system of statutes and regulations adopted since the close of the late war, for raising a revenue in America—extending the powers of courts of admiralty and vice-admiralty—trying persons in Great Britain for offences alledged to be committed in America—affecting the province of Massachusetts-bay, and altering the government and extending the limits of Quebec; by the abolition of which system, the harmony between Great-Britain and these colonies so necessary to the happiness of both and so ardently desired by the latter, and the usual intercourses will be immediately restored. In the magnanimity and justice of your majesty and parliament we confide, for a redress of our other grievances, trusting, that when the causes of our apprehensions are removed, our future conduct will prove us not unworthy of the regard, we have been accustomed, in our happier days, to enjoy. For appealing to that being who searches thoroughly the hearts of his creatures, we solemnly profess, that our councils have been influenced by no other motive, than a dread of impending destruction.

Permit us then, most gracious sovereign, in the name of all your faithful people in America, with the utmost humility to implore you, for the honour of Almighty God, whose pure religion our enemies are undermining; for your glory, which can be advanced only by rendering your subjects happy and keeping them united; for the interests of your family depending on an adherence to the principles that enthroned it; for the safety and welfare of your kingdoms and dominions threatened with almost unavoidable dangers and distresses; that your majesty, as the loving father of your whole people, connected by the same bands of law, loyalty, faith and blood, though dwelling in various countries, will not suffer the transcendant relation formed by these ties to be farther violated, in uncertain expectation of effects, that, if attained, never can compensate for the calamities, through which they must be gained.

We therefore most earnestly beseech your majesty, that your royal authority and interposition may be used for our relief; and that a gracious answer may be given to this petition.

That your majesty may enjoy every felicity through a long and glorious reign over loyal and happy subjects, and that your descendants may inherit your prosperity and dominions 'til time shall be no more, is and always will be our sincere and fervent prayer.

The Olive Branch Petition
(Approved by the Continental Congress on July 5, 1775)
To the King's Most Excellent Majesty.
Most Gracious Sovereign,

We your Majesty's faithful subjects of the colonies of New-hampshire, Massachussetts-bay, Rhode island and Providence plantations, Connecticut, New-York, New-Jersey, Pennsylvania, the counties of New Castle, Kent and Sussex on Delaware, Maryland, Virginia, North Carolina and South Carolina, in behalf of ourselves and the inhabitants of these colonies, who have deputed us to represent them in general Congress, entreat your Majesty's gracious attention to this our humble petition.

The union between our Mother Country and these colonies, and the energy of mild and just government, produced benefits so remarkably important, and afforded such an assurance of their permanency and increase, that the wonder and envy of other Nations were excited, while they beheld Great Britain riseing to a power the most extraordinary the world had ever known.

Her rivals observing, that there was no probability of this happy connection being broken by civil dissentions, and apprehending its future effects, if left any longer undisturbed, resolved to prevent her receiving such continual and formidable accessions of wealth and strength, by checking the growth of these settlements from which they were to be derived.

In the prosecution of this attempt events so unfavourable to the design took place, that every friend to the interests of Great Britain and these colonies entertained pleasing and reasonable expectations of seeing an additional force and extention immediately given to the operations of the union hitherto experienced, by an enlargement of the dominions of the Crown, and the removal of ancient and warlike enemies to a greater distance.

At the conclusion therefore of the late war, the most glorious and advantagious that ever had been carried on by British arms, your loyal colonists having contributed to its success, by such repeated and strenuous exertions, as frequently procured them the distinguished approbation of your Majesty, of the late king, and of Parliament, doubted not but that they should be permitted with the rest of the empire, to share in the blessings of peace and the emoluments of victory and conquest. While these recent and honorable acknowledgments of their merits remained on record in the journals and acts of the august legislature the Parliament, undefaced by the imputation or even the suspicion of any offence, they were alarmed by a new system of Statutes and regulations adopted for the administration of the colonies, that filled their minds with the most painful fears and jealousies; and to their inexpressible astonishment perceived the dangers of a foreign quarrel quickly succeeded by domestic dangers, in their judgment of a more dreadful kind.

Nor were their anxieties alleviated by any tendancy in this system to promote the welfare of the Mother Country. For 'tho its effects were more immediately felt by them, yets its influence appeared to be injurious to the commerce and prosperity of Great Britain.

We shall decline the ungrateful task of describing the irksome variety of artifices practised by many of your Majestys ministers, the delusive pretences, fruitless terrors, and unavailing severities, that have from time to time been dealt out by them, in their attempts to execute this impolitic plan, or of traceing thro' a series of years past the progress of the unhappy differences between Great Britain and these colonies which have flowed from this fatal source.

Your Majestys ministers persevering in their measures and proceeding to open hostilities for enforcing them, have compelled us to arm in our own defence, and have engaged us in a controversy so peculiarly abhorrent to the affection of your still faithful colonists, that when we consider whom we must oppose in this contest, and if it continues, what may be the consequences, our own particular misfortunes are accounted by us, only as parts of our distress.

Knowing, to what violent resentments and incurable animosities, civil discords are apt to exasperate and inflame the contending parties, we think ourselves required by indispensable obligations to Almighty God, to your Majesty, to our fellow subjects, and to ourselves, immediately to use all the means in our power not incompatible with our safety, for stopping the further effusion of blood, and for averting the impending calamities that threaten the British Empire.

Thus called upon to address your Majesty on affairs of such moment to America, and probably to all your dominions, we are earnestly desirous of performing this office with the utmost deference for your Majesty; and we therefore pray, that your royal magnanimity and benevolence may make the most favourable construction of our expressions on so uncommon an occasion. Could we represent in their full force the sentiments that agitate the minds of us your dutiful subjects, we are persuaded, your Majesty would ascribe any seeming deviation from reverence, and our language, and even in our conduct, not to any reprehensible intention but to the impossibility or reconciling the usual appearances of respect with a just attention to our own preservation against those artful and cruel enemies, who abuse your royal confidence and authority for the purpose of effecting our destruction.

Attached to your Majestys person, family and government with all the devotion that principle and affection can inspire, connected with Great Britain by the strongest ties that can unite societies, and deploring every event that tends in any degree to weaken them, we solemnly assure your Majesty, that we not only most ardently desire the former harmony between her and these colonies may be restored but that a concord may be established between them upon so firm a basis, as to perpetuate its blessings uninterrupted by any future dissentions to succeeding generations in both countries, and to transmit your Majestys name to posterity adorned with that signal and lasting glory that has attended the memory of those illustrious personages, whose virtues and abilities have extricated states from dangerous convulsions, and by securing happiness to others, have erected the most noble and durable monuments to their own fame.

We beg leave further to assure your Majesty that notwithstanding the sufferings of your loyal colonists during the course of the present controversy, our breasts retain too tender a regard for the kingdom from which we derive our origin to request such a reconciliation as might in any manner be inconsistent with her dignity or her welfare. These, related as we are to her, honor and duty, as well as inclination induce us to support and advance; and the apprehensions that now oppress our hearts with unspeakable grief, being once removed, your Majesty will find your faithful subjects on this continent ready and willing at all times, as they ever have been with their lives and fortunes to assert and maintain the rights and interests of your Majesty and of our Mother Country.

We therefore beseech your Majesty, that your royal authority and influence may be graciously interposed to procure us releif [sic] from our afflicting fears and jealousies occasioned by the system before mentioned, and to settle peace through every part of your dominions, with all humility submitting to your Majesty's wise consideration, whether it may not be expedient for facilitating those important purposes, that your Majesty be pleased to direct some mode by which the united applications of your faithful colonists to the throne, in pursuance of their common councils, may be improved into a happy and permanent reconciliation; and that in the meantime measures be taken for preventing the further destruction of the lives of your Majesty's subjects; and that such statutes as more immediately distress any of your Majestys colonies be repealed: For by such arrangements as your Majestys wisdom can form for collecting the united sense of your American people, we are convinced, your Majesty would receive such satisfactory proofs of the disposition of the colonists towards their sovereign and the parent state, that the wished for opportunity would soon be restored to them, of evincing the sincerity of their professions by every testimony of devotion becoming the most dutiful subjects and the most affectionate colonists.

That your Majesty may enjoy a long and prosperous reign, and that your descendants may govern your dominions with honor to themselves and happiness to their subjects is our sincere and fervent prayer.

George III's
Proclamation of Rebellion
(August 23, 1775)

Whereas many of our subjects in divers parts of our Colonies and Plantations in North America, misled by dangerous and ill designing men, and forgetting the allegiance which they owe to the power that has protected and supported them; after various disorderly acts committed in disturbance of the publick peace, to the obstruction of lawful commerce, and to the oppression of our loyal subjects carrying on the same; have at length proceeded to open and avowed rebellion, by arraying themselves in a hostile manner, to withstand the execution of the law, and traitorously preparing, ordering and levying war against us: And whereas, there is reason to apprehend that such rebellion hath been much promoted and encouraged by the traitorous correspondence, counsels and comfort of divers wicked and desperate persons within this realm: To the end therefore, that none of our subjects may neglect or violate their duty through ignorance thereof, or through any doubt of the protection which the law will afford to their loyalty and zeal, we have thought fit, by and with the advice of our Privy Council, to issue our Royal Proclamation, hereby declaring, that not only all our Officers, civil and military, are obliged to exert their utmost endeavors to suppress such rebellion, and to bring the traitors to justice, but that all our subjects of this Realm, and the dominions thereunto belonging, are bound by law to be aiding and assisting in the suppression of such rebellion, and to disclose and make known all traitorous conspiracies and attempts against us, our crown and dignity; and we do accordingly strictly charge and command all our Officers, as well civil as military, and all others our obedient and loyal subjects, to use their utmost endeavors to withstand and suppress such rebellion, and to disclose and make known all treasons and traitorous conspiracies which they shall know to be against us, our crown and dignity; and for that purpose, that they transmit to one of our principal Secretaries of State, or other proper officer, due and full information of all persons who shall be found carrying on correspondence with, or in any manner or degree aiding or abetting the persons now in open arms and rebellion against our Government, within any of our Colonies and Plantations in *North America,* in order to bring to condign punishment the authors, perpetrators, and abettors of such traitorous designs.

Given at our Court at *St. James's* the twenty-third day of *August,* one thousand seven hundred and seventy-five, in the fifteenth year of our reign.

God save the King.

An Abridgement of the Prohibitory Act

Introduction: "An act to prohibit all trade and intercourse with the colonies of New Hampshire, Massachuset's Bay, Rhode Island, Connecticut, New York, New Jersey, Pennsylvania, the three lower counties on Delaware, Maryland, Virginia, North Carolina, South Carolina, and Georgia, during the continuance of the present rebellion within the said colonies respectively; for repealing an act, made in the fourteenth year of the reign of his present Majesty, to discontinue the landing and discharging, lading or shipping, of goods, wares, and merchandize, at the town and within the harbour of Boston, in the province of Massachuset's Bay; and also two acts, made in the last session of parliament, for restraining the trade and commerce of the colonies in the said acts respectively mentioned; and to enable any person or persons, appointed and authorized by his Majesty to grant pardons, to issue proclamations, in the cases, and for the purposes therein mentioned."

Article I: "Whereas many persons in the colonies of New Hampshire, Massachuset's Bay, Rhode Island, Connecticut, New York, New Jersey, Pennsylvania, the three lower counties on Delaware, Maryland, Virginia, North Carolina, South Carolina, and Georgia, have set themselves in open rebellion and defiance to the just and legal authority of the king and parliament of Great Britain, to which they ever have been, and of right ought to be, subjects; and have assembled together an armed force, engaged his Majesty's troops, and attacked his forts, have usurped the powers of government, and prohibited trade and commerce with this kingdom, and the other parts of his Majesty's dominions: for the more speedily and effectually supressing such wicked and daring designs, and for preventing any aid, supply, or assistance, being sent thither during the continuance of the said rebellious and treasonable commotions, be it therefore declared and enacted by the King's most excellent majesty, by and with the advice and consent of the lords spiritual and temporal, and commons, in this present parliament assembled, and by the authority of the same, That all manner of trade and commerce is and shall be prohibited with the colonies of New

Hampshire, Massachuset's Bay, Rhode Island, Connecticut, New York, New Jersey, Pennsylvania, the three lower counties on Delaware, Maryland, Virginia, North Carolina, South Carolina, and Georgia; and that all ships and vessels of or belonging to the inhabitants of the said colonies, together with their cargoes, apparel, and furniture, which shall be found trading in any port or place of the said colonies, or going to trade, or coming from trading, in any such port or place, shall become forfeited to his Majesty, as if the same were the ships and effects of open enemies, and shall be so adjudged, deemed, and taken in all courts of admiralty, and in all other courts whatsoever."

Article II exempted ships employed by Britain.

Article III granted the captured ships which were judged "lawful prizes" to the captors—any ship from the thirteen colonies was automatically a "lawful prize."

Article IV provided for the impressment of captured crews into the British navy "as if the said mariners and crews had entered themselves voluntarily to serve on board his Majesty's said ships." If the crews were released, they were to be released somewhere other than in the thirteen colonies.

Article V outlined the procedures for captors claiming their prizes and the basis of determining "lawful prizes." The British government washed its hands of all responsibility in the event of unlawful captures.

Article VI determined that those who claimed to have been captured unlawfully forfeited their ships and further claims if they failed to put up sufficient security.

Article VII required that all papers, books, and ship logs from captured vessels be taken to the admiralty court.

Article VIII provided that captured ships brought to American colonies (other than the thirteen) were to be under the custody of the collector of customs until "divided and disposed of, as his Majesty, his heirs and successors, shall, by proclamation or proclamations hereafter to be issued for those purposes, order and direct."

Article IX provided that no captured prizes be taken to any of the thirteen American colonies.

Article X stipulated fines for judges and officers who failed to execute judgments properly.

Article XI punished officials who acted outside of official capacity by removal from office.

Article XII stipulated the fees to be paid to the officers of the vice-admiralty courts.

Article XIII provided that appeals by either captors or claimants would be made within 14 days after a sentence.

Articles XIV and XV outlined the requirements for making claims.

Article XVI stipulated the penalties for the embezzlement of valuables on captured ships.

Article XVII provided that only duly appointed officers were to appraise and sell the captured ships and goods.

Article XVIII required that government agents register letters of attorney within six months after a judgment.

Article XIX provided further rules for the agents.

Article XX outlined at length the procedures for giving public notice following the sale of captured ships.

Article XXI provided for the punishment of agents and collectors who neglected their duty.

Article XXII required public notification of agents' names.

Article XXIII provided that all duties and customs be paid on all captured ships.

Article XXIV: "Provided always, and be it further enacted by the authority foresaid, That if any ship, vessel, or boat, taken as prize, or any goods therein, shall appear, and be proved, in the high court of admiralty, or vice-admiralty court, to have belonged to any of his Majesty's subjects of Great Britain or Ireland, or any of the dominions and territories remaining and continuing in their allegiance to the King, and under his Majesty's rebellious colonies or plantations before-mentioned, and at any time afterwards again surprized and retaken from his Majesty's said rebellious colonies or plantations by any of his Majesty's ships of war, or other ship, vessel, or boat, under His Majesty's protection and obedience; that then such ships, vessels, boats, and goods, and every such part and parts thereof as aforesaid, formerly belonging to such his Majesty's subjects remaining and continuing under his protection, shall in all cases be adjudged to be restored, and shall be, by decree of the said high court of admiralty or vice-admiralty court, accordingly restored to such former owner or owners, or proprietors, he or they paying for and in lieu of salvage (if retaken from the rebels) one eighth part of the true value of the ships, vessels, boats, and goods, respectively to be restored; which salvage shall be answered and paid to the captains, officers, and seamen, to be divided in such manner as before in this act is directed touching the share of prizes belonging to the flag officers, captains, officers, seamen, marines, and soldiers."

(This article makes it clear that the Parliament acknowledged that protection and allegiance are reciprocal and that the thirteen colonies were excluded from this protection.)

Article XXV prohibited proceeds from captured ships being given to anyone who left the British service without an official discharge.

Article XXVI clarified Article XXV.

Article XXVII required that an accounting of the sales of all prizes be sent to the treasurer at Greenwich Hospital. Some of the proceeds were earmarked for the hospital.

Article XXVIII provided for the punishment of those who failed to give a proper accounting.

Article XXIX required that willful fraud in balancing the accounts be punished.

Article XXX required that letters of attorney be produced by all agents as requested.

Article XXXI required that a list of all such letters be transmitted yearly to the treasurer at Greenwich.

Article XXXII stated further provisions related to Article XXXI.

Article XXXIII restricted the liability of agents.

Article XXXIV provided that the king and his heirs could make further arbitrary regulations respecting the enforcement of the act.

Article XXXV exempted ships which were involved in trade with the thirteen colonies but had already embarked. In some cases this exemption was good until March 25, 1776. After that date any ship trading with the thirteen colonies would automatically be considered a lawful prize.

Article XXXVI gave further provisions related to Article XXXV.

Article XXXVII provided an exemption for ships when two-thirds of the owners resided in England, Ireland, or the West Indies.

Article XXXVIII provided that subjects residing in England, Ireland, and the West Indies could receive goods from the thirteen colonies that were shipped before January 1, 1776. The same subjects would have until March 25, 1776, to collect debts in the thirteen colonies.

Article XXXIX provided further exemptions for trade.

Article XL exempted whale fishermen until March 25, 1776.

(The last several articles were passed in order to protect the commercial interests of the Members of Parliament.)

Article XLI provided that the seizure of persons or ships by customs officials prior to the passing of the act "Shall be deemed just and legal to all intents." In effect, it made all past acts committed by British officials legal.

Article XLII repealed the Boston Port Act of 1774 because it was "rendered unnecessary by the provisions of this act."

Article XLIII provided that the act be in force after January 1, 1776, and that it continue in force "so long as the said colonies respectively shall remain in a state of rebellion."

Article XLIV: "Provided always nevertheless, and it is hereby enacted by the authority of aforesaid, That in order to encourage all well affected persons in any of the said colonies to exert themselves in suppressing the rebellion therein, and to afford a speedy protection to those who are disposed to return to their duty, it shall and may be lawful to and for any person or persons, appointed and authorized by his Majesty to grant a pardon or pardons to any number or description of persons, by proclamation, in his Majesty's name, to declare any colony or province, colonies or provinces, or any county, town, port, district, or place, in any colony or province, to be at the peace of his Majesty; and from and after the issuing of any such proclamation of any of the aforesaid colonies or provinces, or if his Majesty shall be graciously pleased to signify the same by his royal proclamation, then, from and after the issuing of such proclamation, this act, with respect to such colony or province, colonies or provinces, county, town, port, district, or place, shall cease, determine, and be utterly void; and if any captures shall be made, after the date and issuing of such proclamations, of any ships or vessels, and their cargoes, belonging to the inhabitants of any such colony or province, colonies or provinces, county, town, port, district, or place, or of any ships trading to or from such colony or province, colonies or provinces respectively, the same shall be restored to the owners of such ships or vessels, upon claim being entered, and due proof made of their property therein, and the captors shall not be liable to any action for seizing or detaining the said ships or vessels, or their cargoes, without proof being made that they had actual notice of such proclamation having been issued."

Article XLV: "Provided always, That such proclamation or proclamations shall not discharge or suspend any proceeding upon any capture of any such ship or vessel made before the date and issuing thereof."

Special thanks is due Dr. Ian Paisley of Ulster. Dr. Paisley, a Member of Parliament, obtained a copy of the Prohibitory Act from the archives of the British Parliament.
Although the Act is long and vague, two things are apparent:
1. It would be impossible to execute this Act fairly.
2. It would require that the colonies either risk complete financial ruin or unconditionally submit to the British government.

Continental Congress Recommends the
Formation of State Governments
(May 10, 1776)

Whereas, His Britannic Majesty, in conjunction with the Lords and Commons of Great Britain, *has, by a late Act of Parliament, excluded the inhabitants of these United Colonies from the protection of his Crown;* and whereas, no answer whatever to the humble petitions of the colonies for redress of grievances and reconciliation with Great Britain has been or is likely to be given; but the whole force of that kingdom, aided by foreign mercenaries, is to be exerted for the destruction of the good people of these colonies; and whereas, it appears absolutely irreconcileable to reason and good conscience for the people of these colonies now to take oaths and affirmations necessary for the support of any government under the Crown of Great Britain, and it is necessary that every kind of authority under the said Crown should be totally suppressed, and all the powers of government exerted, under the authority of the people of these colonies, for the preservation of internal peace, virtue, and good order, as well as for the defence of their lives, liberties, and properties against the hostile invasions and cruel depredations of their enemies; therefore

Resolved, That it be recommended to the respective Assemblies and Conventions of the United Colonies, where no government sufficient to the exigencies of their affairs have been hitherto established, to adopt such a government as shall, in the opinion of the representatives of the people, best conduce to the happiness and safety of their constituents in particular, and America in general.

The formation of state governments resulted from this recommendation. The recommendation was the direct result of the Prohibitory Act. Notice that the Congress refers to the King as "His Britannic Majesty," not as "Our Majesty." The day after the adoption of this recommendation, John Adams wrote to General Palmer and said: "Yesterday the Gordian knot was cut."

Jefferson's Preamble to Virginia Constitution Adopted June 29, 1776.

WHEREAS *George* the third, king of *Great Britain* and *Ireland,* and elector of *Hanover,* heretofore intrusted with the exercise of the kingly office in this government, hath endeavoured to pervert the same into a detestable and insupportable tyranny,

By putting his negative on laws the most wholesome and necessary for the publick good:

By denying his governours permission to pass laws of immediate and pressing importance, unless suspended in their operation for his assent, and, when so suspended, neglecting to attend to them for many years:

By refusing to pass certain other laws, unless the persons to be benefitted by them would relinquish the inestimable right of representation in the legislature:

By dissolving legislative Assemblies repeatedly and continually, for opposing with manly firmness his invasions of the rights of the people:

When dissolved, by refusing to call others for a long space of time, thereby leaving the political system without any legislative head:

By endeavouring to prevent the population of our country, and, for that purpose, obstructing the laws for the naturalization of foreigners:

By keeping among us, in times of peace, standing armies and ships of war:

By affecting to render the military independent of, and superiour to, the civil power:

By combining with others to subject us to a foreign jurisdiction, giving his assent to their pretended acts of legislation:

For quartering large bodies of armed troops among us:

For cutting off our trade with all parts of the world:

For imposing taxes on us without our consent:

For depriving us of the benefits of trial by jury:

For transporting us beyond seas, to be tried for pretended offences:

For suspending our own legislatures, and declaring themselves invested with power to legislate for us in all cases whatsoever:

By plundering our seas, ravaging our coasts, burning our towns, and destroying the lives of our people:

By inciting insurrections of our fellow subjects, with the allurements of forfeiture and confiscation:

By prompting our negroes to rise in arms among us, those very negroes whom, by an inhuman use of his negative, he hath refused us permission to exclude by law:

By endeavouring to bring on the inhabitants of our frontiers the merciless *Indian* savages, whose known rule of warfare is an undistinguished destruction of all ages, sexes, and conditions of existence:

By transporting, at this time, a large army of foreign mercenaries, to complete the works of death, desolation, and tyranny, already begun with circumstances of cruelty and perfidy unworthy the head of a civilized nation:

By answering our repeated petitions for redress with a repetition of injuries:

And finally, by abandoning the helm of government, and declaring us out of his allegiance and protection.

By which several acts of misrule, the government of this country, as formerly exercised under the crown of *Great Britain,* IS TOTALLY DISSOLVED.

The Unanimous Declaration of the Thirteen United States of America
In Congress, July 4, 1776

When in the Course of human events, it becomes necessary for one people to dissolve the political bands which have connected them with another, and to assume among the Powers of the earth, the separate and equal station to which the Laws of Nature and of Nature's God entitle them, a decent respect to the opinions of mankind requires that they should declare the causes which impel them to the separation.

We hold these truths to be self-evident, that all men are created equal, that they are endowed by their Creator with certain unalienable Rights, that among these are Life, Liberty and the pursuit of Happiness. That to secure these rights, Governments are instituted among Men, deriving their just powers from the consent of the governed, That whenever any Form of Government becomes destructive of these ends, it is the Right of the People to alter or to abolish it, and to institute new Government, laying its foundation on such principles and organizing its powers in such form, as to them shall seem most likely to effect their Safety and Happiness. Prudence, indeed, will dictate that Governments long established should not be changed for light and transient causes; and accordingly all experience hath shown, that mankind are more disposed to suffer, while evils are sufferable, than to right themselves by abolishing the forms to which they are accustomed. When a long train of abuses and usurpations, pursuing invariably the same Object evinces a design to reduce them under absolute Despotism, it is their right, it is their duty, to throw off such Government, and to provide new Guards for their future security.—Such has been the patient sufferance of these Colonies; and such is now the necessity which constrains them to alter their former Systems of Government. The history of the present King of Great Britain is a history of repeated injuries and usurpations, all having in direct object the establishment of an absolute Tyranny over these States. To prove this, let Facts be submitted to a candid world.

He has refused his Assent to Laws, the most wholesome and necessary for the public good.

He has forbidden his Governors to pass Laws of immediate and pressing importance, unless suspended in their operation till his Assent should be obtained; and when so suspended, he has utterly neglected to attend to them.

He has refused to pass other Laws for the accommodation of large districts of people, unless those people would relinquish the right of Representation in the Legislature, a right inestimable to them and formidable to tyrants only.

He has called together legislative bodies at places unusual, uncomfortable, and distant from the depository of their Public Records, for the sole purpose of fatiguing them into compliance with his measures.

He has dissolved Representative Houses repeatedly, for opposing with manly firmness his invasions on the rights of the people.

He has refused for a long time, after such dissolutions, to cause others to be elected; whereby the Legislative Powers, incapable of Annihiliation, have returned to the People at large for their exercise; the State remaining in the mean time exposed to all the dangers of invasion from without, and convulsions within.

He has endeavoured to prevent the population of these States; for that purpose obstructing the Laws of Naturalization of Foreigners; refusing to pass others to encourage their migration hither, and raising the conditions of new Appropriations of Lands.

He has obstructed the Administration of Justice, by refusing his Assent to Laws for establishing Judiciary Powers.

He has made Judges dependent on his Will alone, for the tenure of their offices, and the amount and payment of their salaries.

He has erected a multitude of New Offices, and sent hither swarms of Officers to harass our People, and eat out their substance.

He has kept among us, in times of peace, Standing Armies without the Consent of our legislature.

He has affected to render the Military independent of and superior to the Civil Power.

He has combined with others to subject us to a jurisdiction foreign to our constitution, and unacknowledged by our laws; giving his Assent to their acts of pretended legislation:

For quartering large bodies of armed troops among us:

For protecting them, by a mock Trial, from Punishment for any Murders which they should commit on the Inhabitants of these States:

For cutting off our Trade with all parts of the world:

For imposing taxes on us without our Consent:

For depriving us in many cases, of the benefits of Trial by Jury:

For transporting us beyond Seas to be tried for pretended offences:

For abolishing the free System of English Laws in a neighbouring Province, establishing therein an Arbitrary government, and enlarging its Boundaries so as to render it at once an example and fit instrument for introducing the same absolute rule into these Colonies:

For taking away our Charters, abolishing our most valuable Laws, and altering fundamentally the Forms of our Governments:

For suspending our own Legislature, and declaring themselves invested with Power to legislate for us in all cases whatsoever.

He has abdicated Government here, by declaring us out of his Protection and waging War against us.

He has plundered our seas, ravaged our Coasts, burnt our towns, and destroyed the lives of our people.

He is at this time transporting large armies of foreign mercenaries to compleat the works of death, desolation and tyranny, already begun with circumstances of Cruelty & perfidy scarcely paralleled in the most barbarous ages, and totally unworthy the Head of a civilized nation.

He has constrained our fellow Citizens taken Captive on the high Seas to bear Arms against their Country, to become the executioners of their friends and Brethren, or to fall themselves by their Hands.

He has excited domestic insurrections amongst us, and has endeavoured to bring on the inhabitants of our frontiers, the merciless Indian Savages, whose known rule of warfare, is an undistinguished destruction of all ages, sexes and conditions.

In every stage of these Oppressions We have Petitioned for Redress in the most humble terms: Our repeated Petitions have been answered only by repeated injury. A Prince, whose character is thus marked by every act which may define a Tyrant, is unfit to be the ruler of a free People.

Nor have We been wanting in attention to our British brethren. We have warned them from time to time of attempts by their legislature to extend an unwarrantable jurisdiction over us. We have reminded them of the circumstances of our emigration and settlement here. We have appealed to their native justice and magnanimity, and we have conjured them by the ties of our common kindred to disavow these usurpations, which, would inevitably interrupt our connections and correspondence. They too have been deaf to the voice of justice and of consanguinity. We must, therefore, acquiesce in the necessity, which denounces our Separation, and hold them, as we hold the rest of mankind, Enemies in War, in Peace Friends.

We, therefore, the Representatives of the United States of America, in General Congress, Assembled, appealing to the Supreme Judge of the world for the rectitude of our intentions, do, in the Name, and by Authority of the good People of these Colonies, solemnly publish and declare, That these United Colonies are, and of Right ought to be Free and Independent States; that they are Absolved from all Allegiance to the British Crown, and that all political connection between them and the State of Great Britain, is and ought to be totally dissolved; and that as Free and Independent States, they have full Power to levy War, conclude Peace, contract Alliances, establish Commerce, and to do all other Acts and Things which Independent States may of right do. And for the support of this Declaration, with a firm reliance on the Protection of Divine Providence, we mutually pledge to each other our Lives, our Fortunes and our sacred Honor.

Benjamin Franklin's
Dialogue
Between
Britain, France, Spain, Holland, Saxony, and America.

Britain. Sister of Spain, I have a favor to ask of you. My subjects in America are disobedient, and I am about to chastise them; I beg you will not furnish them with any arms or ammunition.

Spain. Have you forgotten, then, that when my subjects in the Low Countries rebelled against me, you not only furnished them with military stores, but joined them with an army and a fleet? I wonder how you can have the impudence to ask such a favor of me, or the folly to expect it!

Britain. You, my dear sister France, will surely not refuse me this favor.

France. Did you not assist my rebel Huguenots with a fleet and an army at Rochelle? And have you not lately aided privately and sneakingly my rebel subjects in Corsica? And do you not at this instant keep their chief, pensioned, and ready to head a fresh revolt there, whenever you can find or make an opportunity? Dear sister, you must be a little silly!

Britain. Honest Holland! You see it is remembered I was once your friend; you will therefore be mine on this occasion. I know, indeed, you are accustomed to smuggle with these rebels of mine. I will wink at that; sell them as much tea as you please, to enervate the rascals, since they will not take it of me; but for God's sake don't supply them with any arms!

Holland. 'Tis true you assisted me against Philip, my tyrant of Spain, but have I not assisted you against one of your tyrants [James the Second]; and enabled you to expel him? Surely that account, as we merchants say, is *balanced,* and I am nothing in your debt. I have indeed some complaints against *you,* for endeavouring to starve me by your *Navigation Acts;* but, being peaceably disposed, I do not quarrel with you for that. I shall only go on quietly with my own business. Trade is my profession; 't is all I have to subsist on. And, let me tell you, I shall make no scruple (on the prospect of a good market for that commodity) even to send my ships to

Hell and supply the Devil with brimstone. For you must know, I can insure in London against the burning of my sails.

America to Britain. Why, you old bloodthirsty bully! You, who have been everywhere vaunting your own prowess, and defaming the Americans as poltroons! You, who have boasted of being able to march over all their bellies with a single regiment! You, who by fraud have possessed yourself of their strongest fortress, and all the arms they had stored up in it! You, who have a disciplined army in their country, intrenched to the teeth, and provided with every thing! Do *you* run about begging all Europe not to supply those poor people with a little powder and shot? Do you mean, then, to fall upon them naked and unarmed, and butcher them in cold blood? Is this your courage? Is this your magnanimity?

Britain. Oh! you wicked—Whig—Presbyterian—Serpent! Have you the impudence to appear before me after all your disobedience? Surrender immediately all your liberties and properties into my hands, or I will cut you to pieces. Was it for this that I planted your country at so great an expense? That I protected you in your infancy, and defended you against all your enemies?

America. I shall not surrender my liberty and property, but with my life. It is not true, that my country was planted at your expense. Your own records [Prussians] refute that falsehood to your face. Nor did you ever afford me a man or a shilling to defend me against the Indians, the only enemies I had upon my own account. But, when you have quarrelled with all Europe, and drawn me with you into all your broils, then you value yourself upon protecting me from the enemies you have made for me. I have no natural cause of difference with Spain, France, or Holland, and yet by turns I have joined with you in wars against them all. You would not suffer me to make or keep a separate peace with any of them, though I might easily have done it to great advantage. Does your protecting me in those wars give you a right to fleece me? If so, as I fought for you, as well as you for me, it gives me a proportionable right to fleece you. What think you of an American law to make a monopoly of you and your commerce, as you have done by your laws of me and mine? Content yourself with that monopoly if you are wise, and learn justice if you would be respected!

Britain. You impudent b——h! Am not I your mother country? Is not that a sufficient title to your respect and obedience?

Saxony. Mother country! Ha! ha! ha! What respect have *you* the front to claim as a mother country? You know that *I* am *your* mother country, and yet you pay me none. Nay, it is but the other day, that you hired ruffians [Prussians] to rob me on the highway [they entered and raised contributions in Saxony.], and burn my house [and they burnt the fine suburbs of Dresden, the capital of Saxony]! For shame! Hide your face and hold your tongue. If you continue this conduct, you will make yourself the contempt of Europe!

Britain. O Lord! Where are my friends?

France, Spain, Holland, and Saxony, all together. Friends! Believe us, you have none, nor ever will have any, till you mend your manners. How can we, who are your neighbours, have any regard for you, or expect any equity from you, should your power increase, when we see how basely and unjustly you have used both your *own mother and your own children?*

Aids

Many history texts have been surprisingly pro-British in their presentation of the American "Revolution." Therefore, this text includes typical arguments for both views of the key controversies associated with American independence. Also included are two self-exams that are designed to test the knowledge of the readers and students regarding colonial views. The reasons that the colonial leaders gave for believing that resistance and the Declaration of Independence were justified often differ from those given in textbooks. Americans who honor their Founding Fathers should be familiar with the actual justifications they gave for their actions.

Controversy	Both Arguments		Considerations
What caused the growing bitterness between the British government and the American colonies?	Amer.	It is unconstitutional for either the King or Parliament to make laws (other than trade regulations) for us. When British legislation threatens our local assemblies, we will protest and resist.	Colonial charters did not give legislative powers to either the King or Parliament.
	Br.	The King and Parliament are the supreme authority for the whole Empire. Resistance to that authority is unlawful rebellion.	The concept of the British Empire did not develop until after the colonies (over 30) were able to produce profitable trade. The English government had not protected or aided the fledgling colonies.
What was Parliament's role in the colonies?	Amer.	The colonial charters give only supervisory powers to Parliament, not legislative. Parliament was never intended to have legislative powers within our colonies.	Parliament is not mentioned in most of the charters. No legal documents gave the Parliament authority over the colonies.
	Br.	The kings had no authority to grant charters that would not benefit England. Parliament gained supremacy over the monarchs in the Glorious Revolution of 1688 and, consequently, the charters were annulled. Acts of Parliament supersede conflicting colonial legislation.	The authority of a colonial assembly did not extend beyond that colony. Therefore, Parliament was conceded the authority to regulate trade, provided that this authority was not used to interfere with the internal affairs of the colonies.

		Amer.	Br.	
Did Parliament's role change?		A change in a legal relationship requires a legal document. Since there is none, Parliament has no legal authority in America. However, parliamentary regulation of commerce is acceptable as long as Parliament concedes that its authority ends with regulation.	Our constitution does not deny legislative authority in America to Parliament. Any act of Parliament is constitutional as long as it is made in the interests of the Empire.	The British constitution was largely unwritten—based on tradition.
What was the King's relationship to the colonies?		The King has only executive authority. He can exercise veto powers and executive influence but cannot originate legislation. He provides protection and, therefore, we owe him loyalty (which includes fighting in his behalf).	Acts of Parliament are legal expressions of the King's desires. It is hypocritical to claim allegiance and be unwilling to accept royal wishes enacted by Parliament. Submission and allegiance are synonymous.	The unique concept of the separation of executive and legislative powers developed early in colonial America but had not so clearly developed in England. Although the colonists denied that the King had legislative authority in the colonies, they indicated a willingness to accommodate his wishes. But because acts of Parliament rarely originated with the King, they claimed that they were uncertain which acts he supported.

	Amer.	Br.	
Why were British troops in America?	Troops have been kept here since the French and Indian War to enforce unjust legislation, not to protect us. It is an unjustified military occupation.	Refusal to accept parliamentary legislation is in itself open rebellion. Intimidations of the British tax officials justify military occupation.	The colonists believed that they had never been under Parliament's authority. The only legal documents (charters) support this viewpoint. Parliament expressed its belief that it had supreme authority in the Declaratory Act. By 1770 most of the troops were being removed from the frontier. In 1768 regiments were sent to Boston without any explanation.
Was military occupation constitutional?	None of the resistance to illegal taxation can be justly construed as rebellion. We are occupied by a standing army in a time of peace.	Refusing to pay taxes authorized by Parliament is an act of rebellion. The army is needed to protect officials and to keep rebellion from spreading.	A standing army in time of peace defied both the English Bill of Rights and the Petition of Rights—foundations of the British Constitution.
What was the purpose of British taxation?	All of our colonial legislation can be counteracted by parliamentary taxation. Therefore, Britain intends to make us slaves.	The purpose of the taxation is not political control but, rather, economic security for the Empire.	The Sugar Act, Stamp Act, and the Townshend Acts were not regulatory measures. They were designed, instead, to raise revenue from *within* the thirteen colonies. The turbulent political and religious atmosphere in England did not inspire confidence. The colonists doubted that the British government would be a benevolent master.

	Amer.	Br.	
What was the purpose of the monopoly on tea?	The tea monopoly is intended to entice us into acknowledging the supposed right of Parliament to tax us.	The tea monopoly was granted in order to save the East India Company from bankruptcy and to prevent adverse commercial results in England.	The British East India Company was brought to the verge of bankruptcy by corrupt managers—some of whom were officials in the British government. Instead of dealing with the problem, the government granted what the colonists said was an unconstitutional monopoly.
Was taking up arms legal?	We are forced into a difficult decision—either submission to illegal demands or the defense of our constituted legislative independence. We choose to protect the long-established independence of our local legislatures.	The colonial assemblies are by nature subservient to Parliament. Armed resistance to parliamentary taxation is treason.	The British argued that the colonial assemblies were subordinate by nature, but never argued that they were subordinate by law.
Was it a revolutionary war?	We are fighting to preserve our basic institutions, not to change them.	Resistance is armed rebellion and, consequently, the war is a revolutionary war—intended to *establish* independence from Parliament and the King.	The basic institutions changed little after the Separation.

What were the effects of the Prohibitory Act?

Amer.
The King's removal of his protection absolves us of allegiance to him. The Prohibitory Act makes a public declaration of independence necessary.

Br.
Americans have proved their disloyalty by taking up arms. We have removed them from our protection in order to force them to return to their allegiance.

There is little evidence that the colonists wanted independence from the King. Many of their statements have been misconstrued to imply disloyalty when they actually referred to preserving basic legislative independence.

What was the purpose of the Declaration?

Amer.
The Declaration is a proclamation that we will not submit to Parliament by seeking reconciliation. Instead, we will seek help from other countries in defending ourselves against Britain.

Br.
The Declaration announces, not an existing independence, but an independence that the colonists hope to gain through war.

A Self-Examination
(to be taken before reading the text)

1. Who granted the charters to the colonists?
   The King of England granted the charters.

2. In what areas did Parliament have legislative authority over the internal affairs of the colonies?
   Parliament had no authority over their internal affairs.

3. What is the basic obligation of government to its people?
   The basic obligation is protection.

4. Why did the colonists protest the Stamp Act?
   The Stamp Act threatened the colonists' rights to make their own laws.

5. Why did the colonists not want the tea unloaded?
   The colonists wanted to prevent the paying of the taxes. Paying the taxes would have been a recognition of Parliament's supposed authority.

6. What was Britain's purpose in waging war against the colonists?
   The purpose was to force parliamentary legislation upon them.

7. What religion did the Quebec Act establish in Canada?
   It established the Roman Catholic religion.

8. Name the established church of Britain.
   The Anglican Church (Church of England or Episcopal Church) was the established church.

9. What does it mean to be the established church?
   An established church is an arm of the government.

10. To whom was the Olive Branch Petition written?
    It was written to the King of England.

11. Have you ever heard of the Prohibitory Act?

12. If so, what did it do?
    The Prohibitory Act declared war on the colonists and removed them from Britain's protection.

13. Who wrote *Common Sense?*
    Thomas Paine wrote Common Sense.

14. On what date was the Declaration of Independence officially approved by the Continental Congress?
    It was approved on July 4, 1776.

15. How long had America and Britain been at war when the Declaration of Independence was adopted?

They had been at war for fourteen and one-half months.

16. To whom was the Declaration of Independence addressed?
    It was addressed to the world ("candid world").

17. What, more than anything else, caused the Continental Congress to publish the Declaration?
    The need for aid against Britain was the primary reason for publishing it.

18. What kind of government was formed by the Declaration?
    No government was formed by the Declaration.

19. Name the man who wrote the rough draft of the Declaration.
    Thomas Jefferson wrote the rough draft.

20. Was the colonial effort to work out peaceful agreements with the Parliament and King sincere?
    There is no indication that they were insincere.

21. What approximate percentage of the colonists had wanted war with Britain?
    Almost none wanted war.

22. From what country did the colonists hope to receive aid during the war?
    They hoped to receive aid from France, England's old enemy.

23. In your opinion, are revolutions a necessary part of a nation's development?
    Many seem to have been a hindrance. The so-called American "Revolution" was not a revolution.

24. On what conditions would reconciliation have been possible?
    The conditions were that of absolute surrender.

25. Would you say that American independence was caused by man in spite of God or caused by God in spite of man?
    All history has been determined by God.

A Self-Examination
(to be taken after reading the text)

1. Who granted the colonial charters?
   The King of England granted the charters.

2. How much authority over the colonists was Parliament given in the charters?
   Parliament was given no authority.

3. In what year did the French and Indian War end?
   The war ended in 1763.

4. Name the act which was the first to be enacted for the purpose of taxing the Americans.
   The first act enacted for taxation was the Sugar Act of 1764.

5. What articles were taxed by the Stamp Act?
   Legal documents, publications, and similar articles were taxed.

6. Name the act which was passed simultaneously with the repeal of the Stamp Act.
   The Declaratory Act was passed at the same time that the Stamp Act was repealed.

7. What was the purpose of this act?
   Its purpose was to assert Parliament's assumed authority over the colonies.

8. Name the head of the British treasury who proposed the Stamp Act.
   The head of the treasury was George Grenville.

9. What tax was not repealed when the Townshend Acts were repealed?
   The tax on tea was not repealed.

10. What was the communications network organized by the colonial leaders called?
    The network was called the Committees of Correspondence.

11. What was the purpose behind colonial taxation?
    The purpose was to force the colonists to accept parliamentary legislation.

12. What did the first of the Intolerable Acts do?
    It closed the Port of Boston.

13. Name the act which established Roman Catholicism in Canada and the Ohio Valley.
    The act was the Quebec Act.

14. Give reasons why the colonists feared established churches.
    They feared established churches because of forced tithes (taxation), government appointments of the clergy, and control of education.

15. In connection with the Quebec Act, the realization of what caused colonial resentment and fear?
    The realization that Britain could establish Anglicanism in America caused fear.

16. What was the name of the final petition to the King of England, which reaffirmed the colonists' loyalty?
    It was called the Olive Branch Petition.

17. In what month and year was this petition presented to the King?
    It was presented to the King in September of 1775.

18. How many signers of this petition also signed the Declaration only one year later?
    More than half also signed the Declaration.

19. What was the King's response to this final petition?
    The King's response was the proposal of the Prohibitory Act.

20. Give the date on which the war with Britain started.
    The war started on April 19, 1775.

21. Give the exact date on which the Prohibitory Act was enacted.
    It was enacted on December 22, 1775.

22. The Prohibitory Act was made law how many months before the Declaration of "Independence" was approved?
    It was enacted eight months before the Declaration was approved.

23. Who proposed the Prohibitory Act to Parliament?
    The King proposed it.

24. What did David Hartley, a member of Parliament, call the Prohibitory Act?
    Hartley called it a final separation.

25. What did John Adams prefer to call the act?
    Adams preferred to call it the Act of Independency.

26. What did the Prohibitory Act do?
    It declared war on the colonists and removed British protection.

27. Obedience is reciprocal to what?
Obedience is reciprocal to protection.

28. Meeting the conditions of the Prohibitory Act would have required that the colonists do what?
It would have required that they submit to Parliament.

29. Along with the news about the Prohibitory Act, the colonists also received news about what?
They also received news about the hiring of mercenary soldiers.

30. To whom was the Declaration written?
It was written to a "candid world" (to France in particular).

31. Name the author of the Declaration.
Thomas Jefferson was the author of the Declaration.

32. What was the purpose of the Declaration?
The purpose was to dissolve allegiance to the crown, to solicit foreign aid, to call for information of government, and to prevent reconciliation.

33. According to David Ramsay, how many colonists secretly wished for independence, and how well-known were their feelings?
These colonists were few and their feelings not well known.

34. How did John Adams describe independence?
Adams described it as a monster.

35. Why is it impossible for *Common Sense* to have been the cause of independence?
The colonists did not want independence. Knowledge of the Prohibitory Act made them declare it, not Common Sense.

36. Name the author of *Common Sense.*
The author was Thomas Paine.

37. In what month of what year did the colonists learn of the Prohibitory Act?
They learned of it in February of 1776 (by March 1st).

38. Name the movement which provided the thrust for colonial resistance to Parliament.
The Great Awakening provided the thrust.

39. Name the two leaders of this movement.
The two leaders were Jonathan Edwards and George Whitefield.

40. More than anything else, colonial resistance was an effort to preserve what?
It was an effort to preserve religious freedom.

41. The growth of which two Protestant denominations caused Virginia to favor resistance to parliamentary control?
The two denominations were the Presbyterian and the Baptist denominations.

42. What form of government was established by the Declaration?
It established no form of government.

43. The actions of the British government in what country gave the Americans good reason to fear Britain?
The actions in Ireland caused colonial fear.

44. Why does the Declaration hold the King responsible for colonial grievances but the petitions do not?
The King personally proposed the Prohibitory Act after receiving the petitions.

45. What seems to be the best explanation for the Prohibitory Act?
The best explanation seems to be that God used it to make America independent.

NOTES
Chapter One
Colonial Relationship to Britain

[1]Albert Henry Smyth, ed., *The Writings of Benjamin Franklin,* VI (New York: The Macmillan Company, 1907), pp. 412-419.

[2]William MacDonald, ed., *Documentary Source Book of American History, 1606-1926* (New York: Burt Franklin, 1968), p. 7.

[3]Ibid., p. 8.

[4]Ibid., p. 12.

[5]Ibid.

[6]Ibid., p. 16.

[7]Ibid., pp. 20-22.

[8]Ibid., p. 25.

[9]Ibid., p. 34.

[10]Ibid., p. 38.

[11]Ibid., pp. 40-41.

[12]Ibid., pp. 60-62.

[13]Ibid., pp. 44-45.

[14]Ibid., p. 80.

[15]Herbert Butterfield, *George III and the Historian* (New York: The Macmillan Company, 1959), p. 43.

[16]Stanley Ayling, *George The Third* (New York: Alfred A. Knopf, 1972), p. 58.

[17]Ibid., p. 52

[18]Ibid., pp. 448-56.

[19]Ibid., p. 189.

[20]William Edward Hartpole Lecky, *History of England in the Eighteenth Century,* III (London: Longmans, Green and Company, 1883), pp. 16-19.

[21]Thomas A. Bailey and David M. Kennedy, *The American Pageant: A History of the Republic,* I (Lexington, Massachusetts: D. C. Heath and Company, 1979), p. 103.

[22]John Phillip Reid, *In a Defiant Stance* (The Pennsylvania State University Press, 1977). The entire book compares the British government in Ireland with that in colonial America, but pages 152-55 particularly deal with the tyranny of British government in Ireland.

[23]G. B. Warden, *Boston 1689-1776* (Boston: Little, Brown and

Company, 1970), pp. 270-273. These pages discuss the letters and contain the quotations.

[24]J. R. Pole, *Foundations for American Independence* (Indianapolis: Bobbs-Merrill, 1972), p. 26.

[25]Ayling, pp. 113-14.

[26]Oliver M. Dickerson, *The Navigation Acts and the American Revolution* (1951; rpt. New York: Octagon Books, 1974), p. 295.

[27]Donald Barr Chidsey, *The Great Separation* (New York: Crown Publishers, Inc., 1965), pp. 28-29.

[28]Thomas Fleming, *1776, Year of Illusions* (New York: W. W. Norton and Company, Inc., 1975), p. 7.

[29]P. D. G. Thomas, *British Politics and the Stamp Act Crisis: The First Phases of the American Revolution, 1763-1767* (Oxford: Clarendon Press, 1975), p. 53.

[30]Fleming, p. 79.

[31]Dickerson, p. 55.

[32]Chidsey, pp. 70-71.

[33]Ibid., p. 41.

[34]Thomas, pp. 92-93.

[35]Paul Lewis, *The Grand Incendiary* (New York: The Dial Press, 1973), p. 66.

[36]Neil R. Stout, *The Perfect Crisis: The Beginning of the Revolutionary War* (New York: New York University Press, 1976), p. 21.

[37]Chidsey, p. 91.

[38]Howard H. Peckman, ed., *Sources of American Independence: Selected Manuscripts from the Collections of the William L. Clements Library,* I (Chicago: The University of Chicago Press, 1978), pp. 69-113. These pages contain the private correspondence of Barrington and Gage from 1770-1773.

[39]John Shy, *Toward Lexington* (Princeton: Princeton University Press, 1965), pp. 45-83.

[40]Lewis, p. 193.

[41]Marjorie J. Squire, *British Views of the American Revolution* (Boston: D. C. Heath and Company, 1965), p. 45.

[42]Wesley S. Griswold, *The Night the Revolution Began: The Boston Tea Party* (Brattleboro, Vermont: Stephen Green Press, 1972), p. 9.

[43]Squire, p. 74.

[44]Peter N. Carroll, ed., *Religion and the Coming of the American Revolution* (Waltham, Massachusetts: Ginn-Blaisdell, A Xerox Company, 1970), p. 83.

Chapter Two
Colonial Resistance to Parliament

[1]Gordon S. Wood, "Rhetoric and Reality in the American Revolution," *William and Mary Quarterly,* 3rd Series, 23 (January 1966), p. 32.

[2]Jack P. Greene and William G. McLoughlin, *Preachers and Politicians: Two Essays on the Origins of the American Revolution* (Worchester: American Antiquarian Society, 1977), p. 48.

[3]Ibid., p. 45.

[4]Ibid., p. 50.

[5]Peter N. Carroll, ed., *Religion and the Coming of the American Revolution* (Waltham, Massachusetts: Ginn-Blaisdell, A Xerox Company, 1970), p. xii.

[6]Ibid., p. 83.

[7]Ibid., p. 29.

[8]Ezra Stiles, "A Discourse on the Christian Union," in *Religion and the Coming of the American Revolution,* ed. Peter N. Carroll (Waltham, Massachusetts: Ginn-Blaisdell, A Xerox Company, 1970), pp. 69-70.

[9]Ibid., p. 80.

[10]Jonathan Mayhew, "A Discourse Concerning Unlimited Submission and Non-Resistance to the Higher Powers," in *The Pulpit of the American Revolution,* ed. John Wingate Thornton (1860; rpt. New York: Burt Franklin, 1970), p. 49.

[11]Joseph Emerson, "A Thanksgiving-Sermon Preached at Pepperrell, July 24, 1766," in *Religion and the Coming of the American Revolution,* ed. Peter N. Carroll (Waltham, Massachusetts: Ginn-Blaisdell, A Xerox Company, 1970), pp. 87-88.

[12]Samuel Langdon, "Government Corrupted by Vice, and Recovered by Righteousness," in *The Pulpit of the American Revolution,* ed. John Wingate Thornton (1860; rpt. New York: Burt Franklin, 1970), p. 238.

[13]Ibid., p. 245.

[14]Charles Chauncy, "A Letter to a Friend Containing Remarks on Certain Passages in a Sermon Preached by the Right Reverend Father in God, John Lord Bishop of Landoff," in *Religion and the Coming of the American Revolution,* ed. Peter N. Carroll (Waltham, Massachusetts: Ginn-Blaisdell, A Xerox Company, 1970), pp. 95-101.

[15]Ibid., p. 100.

[16]Joseph Perry, "A Sermon Preached before the General Assembly of the Colony of Connecticut . . . May 11, 1775," in *Religion and*

the Coming of the American Revolution, ed. Peter N. Carroll (Waltham, Massachusetts: Ginn-Blaisdell, A Xerox Company, 1970), pp. 124-25.

[17]Ibid., p. 125.

[18]David Jones, "Defensive War in a just Cause SINLESS. A Sermon Preached On the Day of the Continental Fast," in *Religion and the Coming of the American Revolution,* ed. Peter N. Carroll (Waltham, Massachusetts: Ginn-Blaisdell, A Xerox Company, 1970), pp. 143-44.

[19]Steward M. Robinson, *"And ... We Mutually Pledge"* (New Canaan, Connecticut: The Long House, Inc., 1964), p. 68.

[20]Ibid., p. 54, and notes to chapter three.

[21]Carroll, p. xiv.

[22]Robinson, p. 54.

[23]William Cathcart, *Baptist Patriots and the American Revolution* (1876; rpt. Grand Rapids, Michigan: Guardian Press, 1976), p. 87.

[24]Ibid., p. 89.

[25]Carroll, p. xi.

[26]Greene and McLoughlin, p. 48.

[27]Ibid., p. 52.

[28]Lester Douglas Joyce, *Church and Clergy in the American Revolution* (New York: Exposition Press, Inc., 1966), p. 43.

[29]Mark A. Noll, *Christians in the American Revolution* (Washington: Christian University Press, 1977), p. 30.

[30]Ibid., p. 37.

[31]Ibid., p. 39.

[32]L. Tyerman, *The Life of the Rev. George Whitefield,* II (London: Hodder and Stoughton, 1890), p. 632.

[33]Ibid., p. 623.

[34]James H. Hutson, ed., *A Decent Respect to the Opinion of Mankind: Congressional State Papers 1774-1776* (Washington: Library of Congress, 1975), p. 76.

[35]Ibid., p. 78.

[36]Ibid., pp. 78-79.

[37]Ibid., pp. 79-80.

[38]Ibid.

[39]Albert Henry Smyth, ed., *The Writings of Benjamin Franklin,* VI (New York: The Macmillan Company, 1907), pp. 379-80.

[40]George Bancroft, *History of the United States of America,* IV

(New York: D. Appleton and Company, 1885), p. 172.

[41]Ibid., p. 362.

[42]Hutson, p. 130.

[43]Ibid., p. 126.

[44]Charles Callan Tansill, ed., *The Making of the American Republic: The Great Documents, 1774-1789* (New Rochelle: Arlington House, n.d.), p. 16.

[45]Peter Force, *American Archives, Fourth Series,* V (Washington: 1840), p. 50.

[46]Ibid.

Chapter Three
Britain's Response to Colonial Resistance

[1]Curtis P. Nettels, *George Washington and American Independence* (Boston: Little, Brown and Company, 1951), p. 3.

[2]Ibid.

[3]Alfred Henry Smyth, ed., *The Writings of Benjamin Franklin,* VI, (New York: The Macmillan Company, 1907), pp. 311-12.

[4]Thomas Fleming, *1776: Year of Illusions* (New York: W. W. Norton and Company, Inc., 1975), p. 109.

[5]Nettels, p. 24.

[6]Ibid., p. 44.

[7]See the Proclamation in Section VII.

[8]Peter Force, *American Archives, Fourth Series,* III (Washington: 1840), p. 1943.

[9]Ibid., pp. 1943-44.

[10]Marjorie J. Squire, *British Views of the American Revolution* (Boston: D. C. Heath and Company, 1965), p. 23.

[11]Ibid., p. 106.

[12]Lawrence Henry Gipson, *The Triumphant Empire: Britain Sails Into the Storm,* XII (New York: Alfred A. Knopf, Inc., 1965), p. 341.

[13]Force, VI, pp. 186-237. These pages fully discuss this act. Force heads this section "Lord North's Proposed Prohibitory Act."

[14]Danby Pickering, *Statutes at Large,* Vol. 31, pp. 135-36. This is a bookseller's edition. It is the only known American source that contains the entire Prohibitory Act.

[15]Ibid., p. 145.

[16]William Cobbett, *Parliamentary History of England,* Vol. 18, p. 1028.

[17]Pickering, p. 154.

[18]Cobbett, p. 1029.

[19]Ibid.

[20]Ibid., p. 1032.

[21]Ibid., p. 1033.

[22]Ibid., p. 1035.

[23]Ibid., p. 1036.

[24]Ibid., p. 1038.

[25]Ibid., pp. 1038-41.

[26]Ibid., pp. 1103-04.

[27]Force, VI, p. 235.

[28]Cobbett, p. 1105.

[29]George Otto Trevelyan, *The American Revolution,* II (New York: Longmans, Green and Company, 1922), p. 68.

[30]Mercy Warren, *History of the Rise, Progress, and Termination of the American Revolution* (New York: AMS Press, Inc., 1970), p. 279.

[31]Gipson, pp. 348-49.

[32]Benson J. Lossing, *The Pictorial Field-Book of the Revolution,* I (New York: Harper and Brothers, Publishers, 1850), p. 588.

[33]Ibid.

[34]Weldon A. Brown, *Empire or Independence: A Study in the Failure of Reconciliation* (Port Washington, New York: 1941; rpt. Kennikat Press, Inc., 1966), p. 125. This is an interesting study of reconciliation attempts by England before, during, and after the Prohibitory Act.

[35]Force, II, pp. 968-70.

Chapter Four
Colonial Reaction to the Prohibitory Act

[1]Peter Force, *American Archives, Fourth Series,* V (Washington: 1840), p. 1508.

[2]Allen French, *The First Year of the American Revolution* (New York: Octagon Books, Inc., 1968), p. 568.

[3]Julian P. Boyd, ed., *The Papers of Thomas Jefferson, 1760-1776,*

I (Princeton: Princeton University Press, 1950), pp. 338-40.

[4] Ibid.

[5] Ibid., p. 311.

[6] Ibid., p. 312.

[7] Ibid., p. 313.

[8] Edward Dumbauld, *The Declaration of Independence and What It Means Today* (Norman: University of Oklahoma Press, 1950), p. 141.

[9] Carl Becker, *The Declaration of Independence* (New York: Alfred A. Knopf, 1953), p. 203.

[10] Boyd, pp. 290-91.

[11] Jared Sparks, ed., *The Works of Benjamin Franklin,* V (London: Benjamin Franklin Stevens, 1882), p. 107.

[12] Ibid.

[13] David Ramsay, "The View from Inside," in *The Ambiguity of the American Revolution,* ed., Jack P. Greene (New York: Harper and Row Publishers, Inc., 1968), pp. 36-37.

[14] G. B. Warden, *Boston 1689-1776* (Boston: Little, Brown and Company, 1970), p. 283.

[15] Ibid.

[16] Albert Henry Smyth, ed., *The Writings of Benjamin Franklin,* VI (New York: The Macmillan Company, 1907), p. 323.

[17] Paul Leicester Ford, ed., *The Works of Thomas Jefferson,* I (New York: The Knickerbocker Press, 1904), p. 41.

[18] Ibid., p. 25.

[19] Ibid., pp. 25-28.

[20] Charles Francis Adams, *The Works of John Adams, Second President of United States,* I (Boston: Little, Brown and Company, 1856), p. 207.

[21] Ibid., p. 205.

[22] Thomas Fleming, *1776: Year of Illusions* (New York: W. W. Norton and Company, Inc., 1975), p. 125.

[23] Marjorie J. Squire, *British Views of the American Revolution* (Boston: D. C. Heath and Company, 1965), p. 119.

[24] Boyd, pp. 494-95.

[25] John Drayton, *Memoirs of the American Revolution as Relating to the State of South Carolina* (reprinted by the *New York Times* and Arno Press, 1969), pp. 177-78.

[26] Ibid., pp. 180-81.

[27] Ibid., pp. 186-89.

[28]Ibid., p. 254.
[29]Ibid., p. 264.
[30]Ibid., p. 270.
[31]Ibid., p. 271.
[32]Ibid., p. 273.
[33]Ibid., p. 274.

Chapter Five
Neglect of the Prohibitory Act

[1]J. R. Pole, *Foundations for American Independence* (Indianapolis: Bobbs-Merrill, 1972), p. 79.

[2]George Bancroft, *History of the United States of America,* IV (New York: D. Appleton and Company, 1885), p. 343.

[3]Howard H. Peckman, *Sources of American Independence,* II (Chicago: The University of Chicago Press, 1978), pp. 464-67.

[4]Ibid.

[5]*Boston Gazette,* 11 March 1776 (Readex Microprint Mass. 512).

[6]Ibid.

[7]Ibid., 18 March 1776.

[8]Ibid., 25 March 1776.

[9]Ibid.

[10]Ibid., 1 April 1776.

[11]Ibid., 8 April 1776.

[12]Ibid.

[13]Bancroft, p. 290.

[14]Ibid., p. 343.

[15]Emma Willard, *History of the United States, or Republic of America* (New York: White, Gallaher and White, 1828), p. 167.

[16]Elroy McKendree Avery, *A History of the United States and Its People,* V (Cleveland: The Burrows Brothers Company, 1908), p. 318.

[17]Sydney George Fisher, *The Struggle for American Independence,* I (Philadelphia: J. B. Lippincott Company, 1908), p. 438.

[18]Ibid., p. 439.

[19]Ibid., p. 440.

[20]Ibid., p. 441.

[21]Ibid.

[22]Carl Becker, *The Declaration of Independence: A Study in the History of Political Ideas* (New York: Alfred A. Knopf, 1953), pp. 127-28.

[23]George G. Suggs, ed., *Perspectives on the American Revolution* (Southern Illinois University Press for Southeast Missouri State University, 1977), pp. 34-35. The quotations are taken from pp. 34-35, but pp. 13-35 should be read for a full discussion. This is a publication of a lecture given at Southeast Missouri State University.

[24]Ibid.

[25]Norman A. Graebner, Gilbert C. Fite, and Philip L. White, *A History of the American People* (New York: McGraw-Hill Book Co., 1975), p. 90.

[26]John Richard Alden, *The American Revolution, 1775-1783* (New York: Harper and Row, Publishers, 1954), pp. 65-66.

[27]Ibid., p. 67.

[28]David Hawke, *The Colonial Experience* (Indianapolis: The Bobbs-Merrill Co., Inc., 1966), p. 587.

[29]Allen French, *The First Year of the American Revolution* (New York: Octagon Books, Inc., 1968), p. 568.

[30]Curtis P. Nettels, *The Roots of American Civilization* (New York: Appleton-Century-Crofts, 1963), p. 655.

[31]Marshall Smelser, *The Winning of Independence* (Chicago: Quadrangle Books, 1972), p. 77.

[32]Ibid., p. 93.

[33]Ibid., p. 133.

[34]Weldon A. Brown, *Empire or Independence: A Study in the Failure of Reconciliation* (1941; rpt. Port Washington, New York: Kennikat Press, Inc., 1966), pp. 76-77, 290-91.

[35]Richard N. Current, T. Harry Williams, and Frank Freidel, *American History: A Survey* (New York: Alfred A. Knopf, 1971), p. 113.

[36]Henry Steele Commager and Richard B. Morris, *The Spirit of 'Seventy-Six'* (New York: The Bobbs-Merrill Co., Inc., 1958), p. 228. The remark is made in the introduction to the chapter titled "A Great Empire and Little Minds."

[37]Henry Steele Commager, *Documents of American History* (New York: Appleton, 1968).

[38]Edmund Cody Burnett, *The Continental Congress* (New York: The Macmillan Co., 1941), p. 138.

[39]Cornelia Meigs, *The Violent Men* (New York: The Macmillan

Co., 1949), p. 178.

[40]Ibid., p. 207.

[41]George F. Scheer and Hugh F. Rankin, *Rebels and Redcoats* (New York: The World Publishing Co., 1957), p. 149.

[42]Thomas Fleming, *1776: Year of Illusions* (New York: W. W. Norton and Company, Inc., 1975), pp. 65-87.

Chapter Six
Conclusion

[1]Robert E. Brown, *Middle-Class Democracy and the Revolution in Massachusetts, 1691-1780* (Ithaca: Cornell University Press, 1955), p. 401.

[2]Carl N. Degler, *Out of Our Past: The Forces That Shaped Modern America* (1959; rpt. New York: Harper and Row, Publishers, 1970), p. 82.

[3]Neil R. Stout, *The Perfect Crisis: The Beginning of the Revolutionary War* (New York: New York University Press, 1976), p. 18.

[4]Jesse Lemish, "The history of the powerless, the inarticulate, the poor has not yet begun to be written," in *The American Revolution: The Search for Meaning,* ed. Richard J. Hooker (New York: John Wiley and Sons, Inc., 1970), p. 152.

[5]Gordon S. Wood, "We may be approaching a crucial juncture in our writing about the Revolution," in *The American Revolution: The Search for Meaning,* ed. Richard J. Hooker (New York: John Wiley and Sons, Inc., 1970), p. 121.

[6]Martin Diamond, Irving Kristol and G. Warren Nutter, *The American Revolution: Three Views* (New York: American Brands, Inc., 1975), p. 31.

[7]Ibid., p. 35.

[8]George Bancroft, *History of the United States of America,* IV (New York: D. Appleton and Company, 1885), p. 118.

[9]Charles A. Beard, *An Economic Interpretation of the Constitution of the United States* (New York: The Macmillan Company, 1941).

[10]George Bancroft, *History of the United States of America,* Six Volumes (New York: D. Appleton and Company, 1885).

[11]Perry Miller, *The New England Mind* (Cambridge: Harvard University Press, 1954).

Gene Fisher: Having served as a Christian school administrator and as a history teacher at Bob Jones Academy and University for over twenty years, Mr. Fisher has had a lifelong involvement in Christian education. He holds a bachelor's degree from Bob Jones University, a master's degree from Ball State University, and has done graduate work at New York University.

Glen Chambers: Mr. Chambers, a veteran Christian school teacher, is currently a member of the team developing Heritage Studies texts at Bob Jones University Press. He holds a bachelor's degree from Bob Jones University and has done graduate work at the University of Northern Colorado.

The two authors have collaborated on a high school text, *United States History for Christian Schools*™ by Bob Jones University Press. This study on the American Revolution draws on their research for that book.